From Illusion to Reality

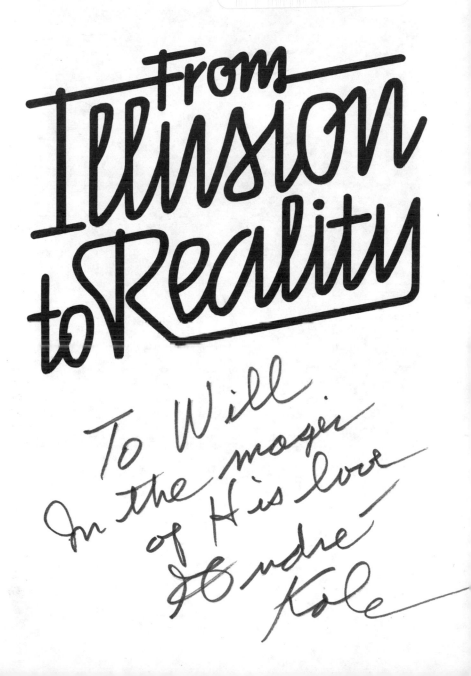

To Will
In the magic
of His love
André
Kole

This fiery arch has become André Kole's trademark.

From Illusion to Reality

Here's Life
Publishers
P.O. Box 1576, San Bernardino, CA 92402

FROM ILLUSION TO REALITY

By André Kole
with Al Janssen

A Campus Crusade for Christ Book

Published by
HERE'S LIFE PUBLISHERS, INC.
P.O. Box 1576
San Bernardino, California 92402

Library of Congress Catalogue Card 84-070482
ISBM 0-86605-146-5
HLP Product No. 403287

Second printing
FOR MORE INFORMATION, WRITE:

L.I.F.E. — P.O. Box A399, Sydney South 2000, Australia
Campus Crusade for Christ of Canada — Box 300, Vancouver, B.C., V6C 2X3, Canada
Campus Crusade for Christ — 103 Friar Street, Reading RGI IEP, Berkshire, England
Lay Institute for Evangelism — P.O. Box 8786, Auckland 3, New Zealand
Great Commission Movement of Nigeria — P.O. Box 500, Jos, Plateau State Nigeria, West Africa
Life Ministry — P.O. Box/Bus 91015, Auckland Park 2006, Republic of South Africa
Campus Crusade for Christ International — Arrowhead Springs, San Bernardino, CA 92414, U.S.A.

CONTENTS

Preface   7

Acknowledgments   9

1. How Do You Explain? 11

2. A Search For Real Magic 21

3. Do Dead Men Speak? 29

4. How Psychic Surgeons Operate 41

5. How Powerful Is the Mind? 51

6. Predicting the Future 61

7. Not So Mysterious Mysteries 73

8. Look Into My Eyes 83

9. Magician or God? 91

10. Called to Serve 103

11. Real Power 113

12. Is Prayer Magic? 121

13. The Ultimate Test 129

14. Faith Healing Versus Divine Healing 137

15. Finding Ultimate Reality 145

Notes 151

PREFACE

Nearly every week, thousands enjoy "The World of Illusion." In this two-hour stage show, I supposedly contact the spirit world, read with my fingers while I'm blindfolded, reveal the mystery of the Bermuda Triangle and levitate high above the stage. But I am always careful to explain that what is seen is just a very well-done trick or illusion

Such a performance inevitably leads to questions from the audience. Many wonder about the reality of psychic phenomena. They want to know how prophets like Jeane Dixon predict the future and how mind readers develop their powers of ESP. They inquire about hypnosis, the potential of the human mind, the chances of contacting the dead or the dead returning, faith healing, and the possibility of knowing God.

Today's thinking person demands to know the truth beyond the stark events that blitz his mind. For this reason, I have made it both a profession and an avocation to investigate the paranormal and intrigues of the 20th century. As an illusionist, I feel that my ability to recognize deception, plus my psychological training and magical techniques qualify me to delve into and explain a number of perplexing phenomena.

In a sense, this book is similar to the long-running TV show "You Asked for It" because it addresses the questions most frequently asked by my audiences. Al Janssen has provided valuable research and writing assistance, and we have tried to give insights into areas that affect most of our lives.

I should state right away that this is not intended to be an in-depth examination of the paranormal. Perhaps as many questions will be raised as are answered. But we hope this book will help you evaluate the stories you read and hear about, and the phenomena you may see or experience but are unable to explain. The books and articles listed in the footnotes will provide much more information should you desire to investigate one or more of these areas further.

ACKNOWLEDGMENTS

I would like to acknowledge several sources and give special thanks to a number of people who have contributed significantly to this book.

I would like to thank Ray Hyman, expert on the paranormal and professor of psychology at the University of Oregon for his input on chapters 5, 6 and 8. Ray also introduced me to the Committee for the Scientific Investigation of Claims of the Paranormal and their quarterly publication *The Skeptical Inquirer* a number of years ago.

Larry Kusche shared his study of the Bermuda Triangle, and Bill Pitts provided valuable insights for the material on UFOs in chapter 7.

Dr. William A. Nolen's book *Healing: A Doctor in Search of a Miracle* provided significant insight for chapters 4 and 14.

My thanks also goes to the worldwide network of magicians. My many friends in this profession have kept me abreast of the latest in unusual happenings and their evaluation of the phenomena.

A special thanks to the one who provides her own sparkling magic in my life—my wife Kathy—and for the encouragement of our children, Robyn, Tim and Stacey.

Finally, special thanks to my friend Bill Bright, President of Campus Crusade for Christ. His encouragement throughout the years has made for honest pursuit and evaluation of the illusion and reality in the world in which we live. He and the staff of Campus Crusade for Christ have provided many insights for chapters 2, 10-12, and 15.

But above all, it has been the request for truth from sincere inquirers and audiences throughout the world that has given me the desire to write about these subjects and made the book a reality.

Chapter one

HOW DO YOU EXPLAIN . . . ?

The small room was crowded and warm. On three sides a fine screen allowed a slight breeze to drift among the observers. Pressed against one screen were the faces of several Filipino natives, each hoping for a glance at the miracle about to take place. On a narrow table lay a young woman draped with a white sheet. She looked up at an overweight, middle-aged man in a colorful native shirt. Surrounding this doctor were several assistants and two magazine reporters from the United States.

The surgeon quietly assured the young woman that she would feel little pain, and if she believed in God's power, she would walk out of that room healed. He opened a Bible to Psalm 23 and read, "Yea, though I walk through the valley of the shadow of death, I will fear no evil: for Thou art with me."[1]

Closing his eyes for a moment, he prayed silently. Then a nurse lifted the sheet and lowered the front of the woman's pants, exposing her abdomen. The doctor took a cotton ball, dipped it into a bowl of water and began to swab a small area of the patient's skin. As he did this, a small amount of blood appeared. Suddenly, he plunged his hand deep into the woman's abdomen, appearing to go almost through her body. A moment later his hand reappeared, holding what appeared to be a piece of diseased tissue. "This is your appendix," the doctor said triumphantly. "You should feel a lot better now."

He dropped the diseased organ and cotton ball in a bucket below the table, rapidly swabbed the area with a clean piece of cotton and covered her again with the sheet. The observers could see no evidence of any incision. As he helped her to her feet, the doctor encouraged the woman to read the Bible every day and to continue to trust God. The whole operation had taken about five minutes.

More than ten thousand people had gathered for a Navajo tribal fair. During the festivities, a half-dozen tribal leaders in

11

full ceremonial dress spread a blanket on the ground. A medicine man threw a dozen feathers into the middle of the blanket, and the leaders sat in a half-circle around it, chanting and beating small drums.

After a few moments, the feathers began to move. Gradually they stood erect on their quills. The Indians, seemingly in a trance, continued to chant and beat their drums while the feathers moved in intricate formations, as a precise military drill team.

In a typical church multi-purpose room in Arizona, fifty high school and college youths gathered for a special program. The guest speaker planned to demonstrate the power that he said could be developed by anyone who trusted God completely with his life.

The demonstration began with two students placing a blindfold over the speaker's eyes and putting tape around the blindfold to ensure that no light entered. Then students produced various objects from their pockets and purses—a comb, pocket knife, wallet. While holding his fingers about twelve inches from the object, the man correctly identified each item.

The students were instructed to write questions on a piece of paper and pass them to the speaker. While still blindfolded, he held each paper in his hand and answered the questions. In some cases he revealed intimate details about that person, though he had never met anyone in the room. At the end of his demonstration, he declared that by blindfolding himself he developed his other senses more keenly. He reemphasized that God gives each one of us special gifts, and we need to discover and use those gifts to help others.

With a loud yell the witch doctor, wearing only a grass skirt and numerous strings of beads, called the natives to the center of the village square. He shouted that the gods had cursed the village because of one man's guilt. Unless the culprit was punished, there would be a plague and many would die. Dramatically he grabbed his rifle and called the offender forward. The crowd withdrew toward their grass-thatched huts and watched in silence as the witch doctor raised his gun and shot once. Blood spurted out of the man's chest and he fell dead.

The dead man was placed inside a crude coffin. Several men dug a grave outside the village, while the witch doctor uttered incantations to break the evil spell on the village. Then the box was buried.

Three days later the witch doctor made another dramatic announcement. The gods were satisfied with the retribution for the unnamed crime, so the dead man could return to the village. All the villagers quickly ran to the grave site, and several young men dug down to the box while the witch doctor chanted. Then the coffin was raised up and set beside the grave. With a dramatic yell, the leader ordered the villagers to open the box. The young man who had been shot and buried for three days slowly began to move. With a dazed look, he sat up and was helped to his feet.

These four stories are just a sample of numerous interesting and unusual phenomena I have encountered throughout the world. Each of them had religious significance, and the feats performed supposedly were evidence of genuine spiritual power.

Since the late 1950s, I have performed illusions in more than seventy countries of the world, baffling millions of people. Yet all of my feats, though perhaps appearing supernatural, are accomplished entirely by natural means. I often say that

André Kole has over a thousand inventions in the field of magic. Here he presents one of his most famous, the "Squeeze Box," in which he squeezes his daughter Robyn down to 1/5 her own size.

13

any eight-year-old can do what I do on stage—with fifteen years of practice! While artistically presenting illusion as reality, I also have studied numerous religions and so-called spiritual feats, attempting to discover if any paranormal phenomena are authentic—if any events could not have been caused by normal, natural causes. I have looked for evidence of genuine ESP, psychokinesis, prophecy, psychic healing and levitation.

In talking with people around the world, I have discovered that most of them believe in God. They also believe that people are capable of displaying special powers from God—what some people would call psychic phenomena. I have concluded from my research and studies as a magician and a psychologist, however, that many of these so-called supernatural incidents are nothing more than sleight of hand.

Take for example the supposed resurrection from the dead performed by the witch doctor, which took place in Liberia. In my investigation I discovered what really happened. The doctor had prearranged the event with his victim, who had placed a balloon full of pig's blood under his shirt. The witch doctor fired a blank from his rifle, and the villager grabbed his chest, puncturing the balloon, and fell over, as if dead.

Once inside the coffin, the man slipped out through a trapdoor in the back of the box, which then was buried empty. When the coffin was dug up, the victim, who had hid for three days, climbed back into it through the trapdoor. Then he simply carried out his performance of being raised from the dead.

What appeared to be a dramatic miracle was only an illusion. But the native villagers were impressed, and were reminded again to follow the leadership of their witch doctor. Such tricks are handed down secretly from one generation to the next, and witch doctors in India and Africa actually have asked me to teach them some of my illusions, so they can increase their influence over their followers.

But villagers in Africa are not the only people being fooled today. Millions of supposedly well-educated Americans are being deceived by charlatans who pretend to have supernatural knowledge or skills. In this book I will examine some of the most common phenomena that mislead people. Based on my research and personal observations, I will answer some of the questions I often am asked after my shows, such as "What do you think about astrology?" "Are there really UFO's?" "Can Uri Geller really bend spoons using only his mind?"

But first, I think it is important to ask why so many people are being deceived. Why do people attend seances, even though it is impossible to communicate with the dead? Why do they listen to seers like Jeane Dixon, whose percentage of correct predictions is no higher than chance? Why do people believe reports of abductions by aliens? Why do so many spend money they can't afford to visit psychic healers in the Philippines, Mexico or Brazil?

I believe that we must understand how people are deceived, so we can discern accurately between what is true and what is false. If there is a God, and if He does give people genuine spiritual power, then it is important to know how to identify that power and separate it from fraudulence. I believe there are five basic reasons why people are misled.

First, *the media has blown many stories out of proportion.*

Tabloid publications such as *National Enquirer* and *Globe* regularly print articles under sensational headlines such as "UFOs: At Last the Proof" and "Amazing Accuracy: Psychic Demonstrates 89% Accuracy." But even respected periodicals can print misleading stories. In May, 1981, *Reader's Digest* published an article titled "New Evidence on Psychic Phenomena." The September/October 1980 *Science Digest* included "Physicists Explain ESP." In March 1980, *Instructor*, a magazine for teachers, ran the story "Your Kids Are Psychic!" with a subtitle "But they may never know it—without your help."

After seeing these articles, a casual reader would assume that ESP is an established scientific fact, but that is not the case. Some articles reveal scientists' uncertainties, but the tone of the headlines and the first few paragraphs lead readers to believe that many people have genuine psychic abilities. Television documentaries can be even more deceiving because they seldom provide enough time to explain all the divergent facts and opinions.

Kendrick Frazier, editor of *The Skeptical Inquirer*, keeps a watchful eye on claims by various publications. In a story titled "Articles on the Paranormal: Where are the Editors?" he explains:

The problem is not of factual inaccuracy. Usually the *facts* are correct. The problem is with the selection process that determines which facts are included and which facts are omitted. Often the facts omitted are those that might weaken a seemingly good story. Hard, skeptical questions are not asked. The overall result is to drastically warp the article's perspective to give a dramatic, but not altogether accurate, view of the subject.[2]

For example, Frazier cites an article in *California Living*, a Sunday supplement magazine in newspapers such as *Examiner* and *Chronicle* in San Francisco and the *Los Angeles Herald Examiner*. The March 9, 1980, article, "The Psychic Body Finders," reports of cases where psychics supposedly helped police solve crimes. Frazier points out the story's shortcomings:

> The hard questions weren't asked: How often do these "psychic bodyfinders" fail? How many guesses do they make before they get one right? And how specific are they? Why do we hear only of the "successes"? And the article makes no mention of the only controlled study I know of that examines the claims of so-called psychic crime-fighters, the one in which the Los Angeles police department found them to be of no use at all in criminal investigations.[3]

This leads directly into my second caution, *determination of the facts is often difficult*.

One of the problems in evaluating reports of unusual phenomena is that only certain facts are selected; unfavorable ones are omitted. Other reports are exaggerated. In some cases, reports actually are fabricated.

I enjoy listening to people try to describe some of my illusions. Once when I was in Madras, India, I appeared to cause my daughter to float within the framework of a large pyramid. The next day, a waitress excitedly told me what some of her customers had said about my show. According to them, I not only had levitated my daughter, but I also had caused her to float out over the audience, turn in a large circle and do several impossible gymnastic feats. Of course, when people exaggerate my illusions, it's hard to tell them that I really wasn't that good!

My good friend David Copperfield made a small lear jet disappear on one of his television specials, but I've heard people

16

say he made a 747 jet disappear while it was flying through the air. Such exaggerations are common and usually unintentional. People easily blow the facts out of proportion, so it is wise to be skeptical about eyewitness reports that deal with any supposed supernatural event.

People also can be deceived by the selection of facts. For example, stories about Bermuda Triangle disappearances sometimes can be explained easily by one piece of information that the writer neglected to mention.

I believe that most editors and writers attempt to be honest in their presentations, but occasionally stories are complete fabrications. Prominent on the cover of the best seller *The Amityville Horror* was the label "A True Story." Lawyer William Weber, who defended Ronald DeFeo, convicted of the slayings of his family in that Amityville house that the Lutz family later bought, said in an Associated Press story, "We created this horror story over many bottles of wine that George Lutz was drinking. We were really playing with each other. We were creating something the public would want to hear about."[4]

Third, *science has difficulty discerning between the fake and real.*

Numerous scientific studies supposedly prove the existence of various paranormal phenomena. Most of these scientists probably sincerely believe in their experiments, and many want to believe that they have verified certain powers. But the facts do not bear them out. First, many experiments cannot be duplicated in other laboratories without widely divergent results. Second, tests that initially produce results significantly beyond the laws of probability produce very normal results when controls are tightened.

One reason scientists often fail to distinguish between illusion and reality is that they do not suspect that someone might try to deceive them. For example, two teenage magicians wrote to the McDonnell Laboratory for Psychical Research at Washington University in St. Louis, Missouri, claiming they had power to bend metal with their minds. For two years the lab tested their powers, verifying their amazing talent. The boys finally admitted publically that they had fooled the scientists.

Why are so many people fooled? Because *the average person*

17

can't detect deception. The best person to detect a trick is an expert in trickery—not a scientist. In my opinion most people cannot distinguish between a genuine paranormal feat and fraud because they aren't trained in the field of deception.

As a magician, I take pride in my profession, and I resent those who misuse our methods, designed for entertainment, to lead others to believe they have supernatural powers, whether they claim it is from God, Satan or some other source. In order to help reveal these frauds, a number of scientists and magicians founded the Committee for the Scientific Investigation of Claims of the Paranormal. The organization promotes careful, controlled testing of those who claim paranormal power, and publishes *The Skeptical Inquirer*, a quarterly journal reporting its investigations.

Finally, I believe *there are probably far fewer genuine supernatural phenomena than generally are supposed.*

But what about psychic healers? Aren't many patients healed? Yes, some are healed. Doctors have demonstrated, however, that as many as 50 percent of their cases are psychosomatic diseases or illnesses that will improve without any treatment, and many illnesses can be healed by suggestion. A lot can be done through the power of the mind. But when it comes to genuine psychic power, I have yet to investigate a demonstration that didn't prove to be the result of trickery.

Since 1966, fellow magician James Randi has carried around a $10,000 check that he will give to anyone who demonstrates one paranormal feat under controlled conditions. So far no one has collected the prize. "With all the claims of paranormal power that we see every day in the press," says Randi, "you'd think that I'd have many more people lined up to take the prize. As it stands, just fifty-two persons have passed the simple preliminaries, only to fail to support their claims to supernatural powers."[5]

During my years of investigation, I have discovered a real spiritual dimension to life, which I also will examine in this book. The evidence for this spiritual life, however, does not come from charlatans who pretend to have supernatural powers. On the contrary, their cleverly learned tricks draw millions of people and dollars *away* from the truth.

It is very easy to be sincere and yet be deceived. I saw this vividly when I was scheduled to do a series of shows in Mexico. A businessman offered to fly me and an interpreter to our various appointments. The pilot did not speak Spanish, and the interpreter did not know much about planes. One afternoon our pilot radioed through the interpreter to an airport tower, informing the controller that we had sighted the runway and were preparing to land. We received clearance and landed, only to be met by a dozen army trucks and soldiers with guns pointed at us. An officer demanded to know why we had landed at the military airport. We then realized that the public airport, with which we had communicated, was on the other side of the mountain. We had believed sincerely that we were landing at the right place, but we were wrong. Similarly, many people follow spiritual leaders because they are convinced they have supernatural powers, but in reality they have been misled.

I have spent most of my life separating illusion from reality, and I would like to share with you some of my discoveries. Perhaps they will encourage you in your search for truth—and protect you from being deceived. You will see that many so-called paranormal phenomena have simple explanations. But before we begin our examination, it is important that you understand a little of my background.

Chapter Two

A SEARCH FOR REAL MAGIC

My summer living quarters were simple—half of a double-car garage, rented from a family in Santa Monica, California. Most of my time out of class was spent in that garage, practicing sleight-of-hand exercises. At that moment, however, the cards and coins lay on the folding table as I rested on my bed. I could feel the blood throbbing at my finger tips, raw from hours of practice. But I ignored the pain as I mulled over an incredible idea.

I was already an excellent magician. I felt that with consistent practice I could become one of the best in the world. It all had started when my mother gave me a "Peter Rabbit Magic Kit" for my seventh birthday. Shortly after that, my father got involved in a business transaction with a magician by the name of Mark Barker—professionally known as Moxo. He showed me a couple of tricks and encouraged me as I began to perform for my friends.

Over the next few years I performed in several states, Canada and Central America, during our extensive family vacations. My father, who was an attorney, a brilliant businessman and civic leader, encouraged me in my hobby, until he realized that it was not just a hobby. Magic dominated most of my waking hours. At school I usually sat in the back row of class and practiced card and coin manipulations while the teacher spoke. The margins of my textbooks and notebooks were filled with illustrations and ideas for new tricks.

I spent hours dreaming of new magical effects and often would not allow myself to go to sleep until I had created at least three new tricks. I studied the great magicians of history, particularly Houdini, the master of escapes. For days I thought about how I might invent an escape more dangerous and daring than any Houdini had attempted. The result was my "Table of Death."

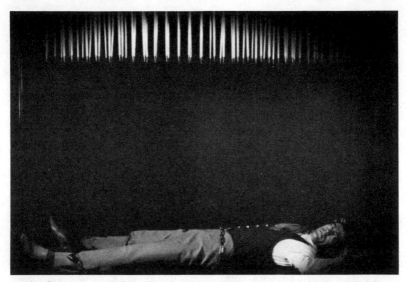

André presents his death-defying creation called the "Table of Death."

In this spectacular illusion, a committee from the audience shackled me to a platform underneath a table of 100 eighteen-inch steel spikes. The table was suspended from a thin rope. After a small curtain was placed between me and the audience, a candle was lit underneath the rope. In twenty to thirty seconds the rope burned through, bringing the four-hundred-pound table of nails crashing down. Then the curtain was pulled back and I was lying on top of the table, reading a magazine.

My first national television appearance—on the original "You Asked For It" show with Art Baker—resulted from this illusion. During this performance one of the spikes broke and flew through the curtain, hitting a cameraman in the head. Fortunately it struck him broadside, not point first, and he wasn't hurt. On another occasion, the spikes fell with such force that one of them was driven clear through a lock. Once I was a little slow to escape and two nails went through my left shoe, but missed my foot.

I prided myself on my creativity. In addition to the "Table of Death," I had invented "Helicopter Cups," which had fooled some of the world's leading magicians, and "Spikes Through a Balloon," which had become the best selling magical trick in history. Now I felt those creative energies surging again as I lay on my bed, staring at the bare light bulb in the middle of the room. How impressive it would be if I concentrated hard on that bulb, and suddenly it exploded! I could do the trick fairly simply and claim that it was the power of my mind.

It would be so easy to deceive people. I could even form a religion of the mind. I could teach about the incredible potential of the human brain and do dazzling feats to demonstrate its power. I would make objects levitate, read and identify objects while blindfolded, and make incredible observations and prophecies concerning my followers. I could do it all through trickery.

My body was alert with excitement as I thought of the possibilities for such a religion. I could easily gain thousands, perhaps millions of believers. I could become fabulously wealthy. The more I thought about it, the more I began to feel a supernatural high, as if spurred by some demonic force.

I pondered these thoughts for several weeks and came up with many ideas for this religion as I practiced manipulation skills. I even began to wonder if it were possible to do some mental feats without trickery. Then one Sunday morning I woke up early and felt a strange desire to go to church. I knew of a church of my family's denomination just six blocks away, so I decided to go there. It was a warm, summer morning, and few people were on the streets, so I slowed my normal quick walking pace to enjoy the weather.

Again I started to think of my idea of forming a religion. All of a sudden I felt a warm, loving presence. It was so different from the thoughts that had captivated me for the past few weeks. I felt almost like a coat was being placed around my shoulders by a friendly, loving person. In that moment, I sensed the presence of God and that He had a plan for my life. In a flash I thought, "Someday, you will be God's magician."

That presence remained with me through the church service and was so overwhelming that I couldn't remember anything that was said or sung. It didn't depart until I returned to my temporary home. From that time on, I had no interest or desire to control the minds and lives of others. I was determined to use magic solely as an art form, for entertainment purposes only.

Even to this day I am unable to find words that adequately describe my experience. People could interpret it in various ways, so I seldom share it. All I know is that what happened made a lasting impact on my life. It also showed me how easily my skills could be abused, if they were not channeled in the right direction.

Today, some of the things I do in my shows create effects that might lead one to believe I have supernatural powers. I constantly have to repeat that *everything I do on stage is accomplished entirely by natural means. I have no supernatural powers.*

That experience in Santa Monica heightened my spiritual desire and for the next few years, I embarked on a personal spiritual pilgrimage. I studied the major religions of the world, but I did not find reality. Nothing in Buddhism, Islam, Hinduism or other religions led me to believe they were anything more than empty rituals I'd seen in most American churches I'd attended.

In college I continued my search for truth. Though magic was my first love, I also desired to investigate how people think. Since universities did not offer a major in magic, psychology seemed a good choice. Perhaps I could learn some useful principles for my shows. So I enrolled in a basic psychology class.

The professor, whom I highly respected, presented answers to my most important questions: "Why am I here?" "Where am I going?" "What is the real purpose of life?" After I earned a degree in psychology, however, I learned that the answers it offered were not really satisfactory. Only two years later, the professor whom I so highly respected committed suicide. What a devastating indictment against what I thought represented an almost holy search for truth.

While I was still in college, I married a beautiful young lady, and I started my own company for promoting and selling some of my magical inventions. I perfected and released a new magical effect each month. Then, for the first five years after graduation, I was very involved in the business world. At the age of twenty-five, I was in charge of the statewide operation of Transamerica Corporation, co-owner of a ranch and partner in a number of office buildings. In addition I did about twenty magic shows a month. By the world's standards I was extremely successful, but I was haunted by a feeling of emptiness. I couldn't understand how, with all my activities and achievements, I could be so tremendously bored.

I felt particularly restless when I walked out onto the stage after a performance, the heels of my shoes echoing through the empty theater. A few minutes earlier I had brought the crowd to their feet in applause. Now they were gone, and I felt loneliness, emptiness. Why had I worked so hard to be so successful? What had it brought me? What more could I possibly accomplish that would fill this emptiness?

I often thought of the true story I heard from a professor of one of my real estate business classes. In 1923, in a large hotel in Chicago, a very important meeting was held with nine of the world's most successful financiers: Charles Schwab, president of the largest independent steel company; Samuel Insull, president of the largest utility company; Howard Hopson, president of the largest gas company; Arthur Cotton, the greatest wheat speculator; Richard Whitney, president of the New York Stock Exchange; Albert Fall, a member of the President's Cabinet; Leon Fraser, president of the Bank of International Settlements; Jesse Livermore, the greatest "bear" on Wall Street; and Ivar Krueger, head of the greatest monopoly.

Twenty-five years later, Charles Schwab had died in bankruptcy; Samuel Insull had died a fugitive from justice, penniless in a foreign land; Howard Hopson was insane; Arthur Cotton had died abroad, insolvent; Richard Whitney had spent time in Sing Sing Penitentiary; Albert Fall had been pardoned so that he could die at home; Jesse Livermore, Ivar Krueger and Leon Fraser had all died by suicide. All of these men had learned the art of making a living, but none of them had learned how to live.

Neither psychology nor success provided the answers. I learned that psychiatrists had the highest suicide rate of any profession. One of my neighbors, a successful businessman, committed suicide. Another businessman whom I saw every day dived head first off the eleventh story of the building where I had my office. A world-famous magician, whom I'd met and admired, literally drank himself to death. Yet, I reasoned, there had to be something that would give some hope, some reason for living.

Then one evening, my wife and I visited a church and were invited to a meeting of young couples. Unlike other religious people I had met, they did not talk about religion or philosophy or a long list of do's and don'ts. I probably would not have listened if they had. Rather, they talked about how they had found a relationship with God that was changing their lives.

I was intrigued, but I had no intention of being deceived by a first-century trickster, if that was all that Jesus was. I took pride in the fact that I had never been fooled by another magician. So, accepting a friend's challenge, I spent several months investigating Christianity from a magician's point of view. I will share more about that investigation in chapter 10.

Intellectually, I concluded that Jesus was who He claimed to be—the Son of God. Jesus could not possibly have used trickery to accomplish what He did, for it would have required several truckloads of equipment, and even then, most of His miracles still could not have been performed by trickery.

I saw further evidence of Christianity in my new friends. These people—students, businessmen, an athletic coach—had a different quality of life, which they attributed to their personal relationship with Jesus Christ. He was alive within their hearts. I started reading the Bible, trying to understand what made them different. I read again about Jesus Christ dying for our sins, which I'd heard about for many years. It still sounded like a lot of hocus-pocus to me, until one night I heard a story about a man who worked on a railroad.

This man's job was to raise and lower a giant drawbridge over a river. One day he took his eight-year-old son with him to work. The bridge was up, as a ship had just gone through, but now a train was coming, so he started to lower the bridge. Suddenly he heard a horrible scream behind him. He turned around and saw that his son had slipped and fallen down among the giant gears of the bridge, and was being crushed.

The father knew that if he raised the bridge, he could save his little boy's life. But he also knew that this would cause the train to crash, killing hundreds of people. He had to make a decision. He chose to lower the bridge and watch his own son die, crushed among the gears. As the train went over the bridge a number of people waved to the father as they went merrily on their way, unaware of the sacrifice that he had made to save their lives.

Likewise, I realized that two thousand years ago, God had watched the death of His only Son on the cross, when He could have stopped the whole thing at any moment. The Bible says, "For God so loved the world [so loved you and me], that He gave His only begotten Son that whoever believes in Him should not perish, but have eternal life."[1]

Another illustration helped me understand the significance of Jesus Christ. It involved a man who was pacing back and forth in front of the gate to the White House. Occasionally he'd stop and ask if there was any way he could see the President to give him a most urgent message. But the guard just shook his head and turned away.

A little boy was sitting on a bench by the gate, watching this take place. As the man continued to pace, the little boy finally walked up to him and asked, "Mister, are you worried about something? Are you in trouble?" The man stopped in surprise, then put his hand on the child's head and said, "Yes, Sonny, I am. I must see the President, but there is no way that I can get to him."

The boy said to the man, "Take my hand." While he was tempted to ignore the boy, he decided to humor him by following his suggestion. With the boy's hand in that of the man, the guard bowed and the great closed gates swung open. The young boy led the amazed man into the inner sanctum of the President's study. Through that boy—the President's son—the man gained access to the President.

I learned that this is exactly how we gain access to God— through His Son. When we establish a personal relationship with Jesus Christ, He takes each of us by the hand and leads us into the presence of His Father.

Finally it all made sense to me. So one day, in the quiet of my own home, I simply prayed, "Dear Lord Jesus, thank You for dying for my sins. Right now I invite You to come into my life. Forgive my sins and make my life what You want it to be. Thank You, Lord Jesus, for coming into my life. Amen."

At that moment, I knew that Jesus Christ had, indeed, come into my life. I was a new person! Shortly thereafter I read in Jeremiah, "You will seek Me and find Me, when you search for Me with all your heart."[2] I knew that at last I had found truth; I had found God.

During the more than twenty-five years since that experience, I have studied many unusual phenomena. For a brief time, I had faced an enticing lure to misuse my talents. I had even considered using those gifts to establish my own evil "religion." Because of that, I have become particularly sensitive to the area of baffling phenomena, and in the next few chapters I will relate my discoveries from my background as a magician and psychologist, and as a Christian. I hope these insights will help you discern between illusion and genuine spiritual reality.

Chapter Three

DO DEAD MEN SPEAK?

What could be more fascinating than to communicate with a person who has died? This would be especially meaningful if you loved that person very much.

During the mid-1800s, dozens of spirit mediums traveled around the United States and England and demonstrated their powers, attracting large crowds. One of the most popular was a slender Irish blond named Anna Eva Fay. She sat inside a large, custom-made cabinet, her wrists securely bound behind her with strips of cloth and tied to a harness ring attached to a post in the rear of the cabinet. When the curtains were closed and the spirits summoned, musical instruments were played, various objects were tossed, nails were hammered into a block of wood, and dolls were cut out of paper. These activities supposedly were evidence of spirits. The spectacular performance concluded when the "spirits" took a knife and cut Mrs. Fay's cords.

The effect was so astounding that thousands flocked to see her demonstrations. An eminent scientist, Sir William Crookes, tested Mrs. Fay, having her place her hands on brass handles that led to a galvanometer. While the galvanometer showed no break in the current, the mysterious manifestations were demonstrated. Later various individuals exposed Mrs. Fay as a fraud, who performed her feats using clever trickery, yet people continued to flock into large theaters to see her amazing performances.

Before her death, Mrs. Fay's secret was passed on to a man from Ireland who later came to the United States, where he and his wife presented the seance. Before their death, they taught it to their son Harry Willard, who presented the seance with his wife for nearly 50 years. They shared it with their daughter Frances, from whom I learned the secret of the Anna Eva Fay seance. I made arrangements for Frances to train my wife Aljeana to present the various kinds of "spirit" manifestations.

For several years we invited members of the audience to the stage to help tie my wife's hands to a post. Then, while she supposedly was in a trance, we closed the curtains on her. Immediately a tambourine played and a basket flew over the curtain. The curtain was closed for less than ten seconds before I reopened it, revealing my wife slumped in the same position, her hands still firmly tied. Then I invited a member of the audience to stand blindfolded inside the curtain. Soon after the curtain was closed, the participant came running out of the cubicle, a bucket over his head and his shoes removed.

We included this unique presentation in our performances throughout the world until Aljeana's death in 1976. It was entertaining and got a lot of laughs, but it also showed how easily people can be deceived. My wife had no power to contact the spirits. Everything she did was an illusion, created exclusively by physical means.

Modern belief in communication with the dead, or spiritism as it often is called, began in America in 1848 in the little town of Hydesville, New York. People began to hear mysterious knocking sounds in a farmhouse. Margaret Fox (age eight) and her younger sister Catherine began asking questions of the "spirit" inside the house, and answers came as distinct raps, apparently from inside the walls. For example, when one girl help up four fingers and asked, "How many fingers?" they heard four raps. Through their questioning, they revealed that the originator of the noises was the spirit of a man murdered in the house several years before. The story spread and people from all over the country came to see this remarkable phenomenon.

For forty years the Fox sisters traveled throughout the world and made a great deal of money demonstrating this spirit's communicative powers. The mysterious rappings followed them wherever they went, and though they were examined by leading doctors, scientists and preachers, no trickery was discovered.

Then in 1888 the girls confessed that it was all a fraud. They had started by tying a string to an apple and bumping it on the floor at night to scare their superstitious mother. She did not suspect trickery since her children were so young. When

30

she called in her neighbors, the girls found a more effective method for producing the raps: They snapped the joints in their toes, in much the same way as one cracks the knuckles in his fingers. In the quiet darkness of a seance room, where a wooden floor served as a sounding board, those raps proved very effective.

A confession by Margaret Fox appeared on September 24, 1888, in the *New York Herald*. Among other things it said, "As far as spirits were concerned, neither my sister nor I thought about it. I knew there was no such thing as the departed returning to this life. I have seen so much miserable deception that every morning of my life I have it before me. That is why I am willing to state that spiritualism is a fraud of the worst deception. I trust that this statement, coming solemnly from me, the first and most successful in this deception, will break the rapid growth of spiritualism and prove that it is all a fraud, hypocrisy and delusion."

Unfortunately the growth in spiritualism continued to mount, even in the face of evidence that these two leading mediums had used trickery.

The great magician Harry Houdini probably was most responsible for exposing fraudulent mediums. During the final years of his life, he was consumed by an obsession to find a genuine medium to contact his mother. Shortly before her demise, their family had been rocked by scandal. His brother Nat's wife had left him to marry another brother, Leopold. Houdini could not forgive Leopold and told his mother that he looked to her for guidance on what he should do.

Houdini was in Europe when his mother died. During her final hours, she tried to give the family by her bedside a message for her son, but could not get the words out. Houdini wondered what his mother was trying to say. Did she want him to forgive his brother? He often visited his mother's grave, begging her to tell him her last words. Only spiritualists believed in communication with the dead, but Houdini believed that all the mediums he had met were frauds. He determined, however, that if a genuine medium existed in the world, he would find him.

During his remaining years Houdini attended some five thousand seances. In many of them, ghostly whispers claimed to be his mother, but there was one problem. The voices were always in English, while his mother spoke only Yiddish. As a result, he became very bitter against these charlatans who impersonated his dear mother, and he began an all-out campaign to expose fake mediums.

He also began making pacts with his friends, vowing that whoever died first would attempt to communicate with the other using a secret code. He lectured about spiritualism around the country, demonstrating common techniques used by mediums, such as table levitation, playing of musical instruments and writing on blank slates. He also offered a $5,000 prize to any medium who could produce an effect that he could not duplicate. No one ever collected the prize.

Houdini wrote two books about his study, revealing the results of tests with the best-known mediums and disclosing techniques they used to gather information and perform various feats. In his book *A Magician Among the Spirits* he concluded:

> To my knowledge I have never been baffled in the least by what I have seen at seances. Everything I have seen has been merely a form of mystification. The secret of all such performances is to catch the mind off guard and the moment after it has been surprised to follow up with something else that carries the intelligence along with the performer, even against the spectator's will ...
>
> I have said many times that I am willing to believe, want to believe, will believe, if the spiritualists can show any substantiated proof, but until they do I shall have to live on, believing from all the evidence shown me and from what I have experienced that spiritualism has not been proven satisfactorily to the world at large and that none of the evidence offered has been able to stand up under the fierce rays of investigations.[1]

Shortly before his death, Houdini and his wife, Bess, made a pact that whoever died first would attempt to contact the other with these words: "Rosabelle, answer, tell, pray, answer, look, tell, answer, answer, tell." The words following "Rosabelle" were a code that spelled out the word "Believe." On Halloween of 1926, Houdini died of a ruptured appendix. Two and half years later, a young medium named Arthur Ford sent to Houdini's widow a one-word message, "Forgive," supposedly from Houdini's mother. A message from her husband followed, with the predetermined words in the correct sequence.

Two days later, Bess met with Ford and heard her husband supposedly speak to her through the medium. News of the event spread quickly and the next day newspapers blared headlines that Houdini had returned from the dead. The great magician's widow signed a declaration that read: "Regardless of all statements to the contrary, I wish to declare that the message, in its entirety and in the agreed-upon sequence, given to me by Arthur Ford, is the correct message pre-arranged between Mr. Houdini and myself." The statement was cosigned by three witnesses.

But was this genuine evidence of Houdini's return? Skeptics doubted it and found ample reason for their suspicions. Raymund Fitzsimons in his book *Death and the Magician* tells how a close friend of Houdini and his wife exposed the fraud to the widow:

> Joe Rinn heard the news and decided that the whole affair was a spook trick to end all spook tricks, a trick that must be exposed. Bess was convinced of the truth of Ford's seances, so Rinn and other friends of Houdini's reminded her of certain things which in her emotional state she had forgotten. Ford's message from Houdini's mother had included the evidential word FORGIVE, but the Brooklyn *Eagle* of March 13, 1927, a year before Ford's seance, had quoted Bess as saying that any authentic communication from Houdini's mother would have to include that word. Ford could have read this. She was also reminded that the code words used had been printed in Harold Kellock's biography of Houdini, published the previous year, on which she had collaborated. Bess admitted that she had not recalled these things. But at the time of the seance she had been sick with influenza and emotionally run down.[7]

Later Bess retracted her statement about Ford, and to her dying day maintained that she had not received any communication from her late husband. Yet the controversy over spiritualism still rages today. Millions of people believe that contact with the dead is possible and spend millions of dollars to communicate with loved ones through mediums.

After numerous exposures of fraudulent tricks used in

seances early in the twentieth century, mediums devised safer techniques. Mental mediums like Arthur Ford became more prevalent. In his type of seance, the medium usually goes into a trance and his or her body comes under the control of a spirit. (Ford supposedly became controlled by Fletcher, the son of a wealthy French-Canadian family. He had died suddenly in 1918 while attending college.) The spirit passes messages from other spirits, through the medium, to the sitter. In order to authenticate the communication, the spirit relates seemingly insignificant details that only the sitter could know or verify.

In his book *The Spiritual Frontier*, William V. Rauscher, an Episcopal priest, compares it to a phone conversation with a very poor connection, in which the operator serves as a go-between. The problem is to determine if your friend on the other end of the line really is who he says he is. To prove that the communication is genuine, the medium relates what appears to be trivial details. This information, which the client believes the medium could not possibly know, proves that contact with the deceased loved one or friend has been established. The argument sounds good on the surface, but ample evidence shows that many mediums keep extensive files about their clients.

In 1967, Ford conducted the most famous seance in recent history. The event was shown on network television in Canada and involved Episcopal bishop James Pike. During the seance Ford supposedly received communications from Pike's son who had committed suicide in February, 1966. Pike was convinced that Ford could not have obtained the facts he gave by any other means, thus supporting his belief that Ford was a genuine medium.

But in his book *Arthur Ford: The Man Who Talked with the Dead*, Allen Spraggett told about his shocking discovery after Ford's death.

> William Rauscher and I, researching this biography, were sifting through Arthur Ford's private papers. Several boxes bulged with the medium's personalia—letters, diaries, books, newspaper and magazine clippings, scrapbooks, even his income-tax returns . . . .We knew that we had not inherited all Ford's papers; an unknown amount of personal material had been destroyed by a former secretary shortly after the medium's death, presumably on his

instructions . . . .

Bill Rauscher was holding a newspaper clipping and, as he scanned it, his face clouded over.

"What's wrong?" I asked.

Without a word, he handed me the clipping.

It was an obituary, undated, from the *New York Times*. The headline told me why Bill Rauscher was disturbed; it read: BISHOP BLOCK, 71, IS DEAD ON COAST.

In the Ford-Pike seance, one of the purported discarnates who communicated on television, in a manner that James Pike found peculiarly convincing, was his episcopal predecessor, the Right Rev. Karl Morgan Block, late Bishop of California.

As I read the obituary my disturbance increased.

The Block communicator had mentioned several small —even trivial—details which Pike considered especially evidential since their very triviality seemed to rule out the possibility of prior research by the medium. The details Pike found impressive appeared to be too obscure, too idiosyncratic, to be accessible to research. However, every one of these supposedly unresearchable items was mentioned in the *New York Times* obituary.[3]

Later the researchers discovered further evidence that most, if not all, of the information Ford gave in his TV seance was obtained through personal research, primarily newspaper accounts. While Spraggett and Rauscher say that this evidence does not discount the fact that Ford was a genuine medium, the truth is that Ford's two most famous seances at the beginning and the end of his career are shrouded in suspicion.

One of the most recent damaging revelations against spiritualism was made by a very successful medium, Lamar Keene. In his book, *The Psychic Mafia*, he details how he conned hundreds of people into believing that he had supernatural powers.

Lamar was raised in a Baptist family and for a time considered entering the ministry. In his twenties, however, he was introduced to spiritualism by a friend. Together they attended a large spiritualist church. After a little more than a year, the pair launched into their own work, half believing they had genuine, though undeveloped, psychic power.

They quickly learned that to develop a following, they

needed to give people tangible manifestations of the spirits. They soon discovered how to do that through a national information network. Mediums kept extensive files on their subjects and, using this network, they could obtain accurate information quickly about a visitor from any part of the country.

Many mediums add physical manifestations, such as apports and materializations, to their messages. Keene was adroit at dropping personal trinkets in the laps of sitters, but relied primarily on the quality of his information, which was culled from newspaper clippings and pilfered from the wallets and purses of unsuspecting clients.

James Randi, in his book *Flim-Flam!*, tells about an interview with Keene shortly after his startling revelation:

> I interviewed him and discovered that he knew little about the more subtle methods of chicanery. He explained to me that he didn't *need* to know much. Anything he did would serve to convince the faithful, he said. They fell for the most transparent ruses, many of which were thought up on the spur of the moment, and he and his fellow charlatans laughed themselves silly, at the end of an easy day's work, as they recounted how simple it had been.[4]

It is interesting that Keene's book was named *The Psychic Mafia*. After his defection from spiritualism, his former friends threatened to kill him. One night, several shots were fired at him from a passing car. He was wounded in the stomach and recovered only after a long hospitalization.

About a dozen companies in the United States specialize in building intricate props that spiritualists use in their performances. Several of these companies have extensive catalogues of items they stock or can build. Most of the catalogues also have a section listing books about spiritualistic tricks.

Recently I went to the shop of a man who was doing some work for me. He was building a spirit vase for one of his other clients, a witch doctor in Africa. A person could whisper a question into this apparently normal vase and a voice, supposedly from the spirit world, would answer in a mysterious whisper from within the vase.

At one time such items were very popular with spirit mediums, but now most people in the United States know what can be accomplished through electronics. You can imagine, though, how such a "miraculous" demonstration of the witch doctor's powers would astound some superstitious natives in Africa.

Despite such obvious frauds, people still ask, "Do the dead return?" After nearly thirty years of studying this question from the point of view of a magician, psychologist and a person deeply interested in spiritual truth, I have to conclude that willful communication with the dead is impossible. That is not to say that all mediums are insincere. Some may genuinely believe that they have the power to communicate with the dead.

When my daughter, Robyn, was a teenager, her boyfriend's mother became very involved with a spirit medium in Phoenix. My daughter attended one of her seances and was frightened by the experience. When she told me about it, I was angry and immediately wanted to confront this woman and expose her racket. On my way to meet her, I realized that my anger and hatred for what she was doing was not the right attitude. I asked God to forgive me and to give me a genuine concern and love for this person.

We ended up talking for several hours and this woman started asking questions about reality, the meaning of life, and the person of Jesus Christ— many of the questions I had asked as a young man. She had turned to spiritualism while looking for answers. Like many mediums, she found that her clients demanded tangible demonstrations of communication with the dead. She had a sincere desire to help people, but felt trapped by her circumstances; she felt forced to cheat and produce spirit forms and other manifestations.

I think people look to mediums for two reasons. First, they have lost loved ones and intensely desire to contact them and establish their existence. The other reason is curiosity, an interest in the unusual and supernatural.

The Bible makes it very clear that we are to avoid any dealings with mediums. In Deuteronomy, Moses told the Israelites:

> When you arrive in the Promised Land you must be very careful lest you be corrupted by the horrible customs of the nations now living there . . . No Israeli may . . . call on the evil spirits for aid, or be a fortune teller, or be a

serpent charmer, medium, or wizard, or call forth the spirits of the dead. Anyone doing these things is an object of horror and disgust to the Lord, and it is because the nations do these things that the Lord your God will displace them.[5]

Why doesn't God want His people to attempt to contact the spirits of the dead? First, such activities distract us from our faith in Him. They may even prevent us from learning about his plan of salvation. Second, most people will misinterpret what they see and hear. They so want to believe that they have contacted a loved one that they easily are deceived by fraud. Third, such communication causes tremendous emotional feelings, with which God didn't intend for us to deal. Once a person believes he has contacted a loved one, he longs to continue the conversation. This can cause serious spiritual and psychological problems.

It is revealing to look at the lives of mediums after many years in their profession. Awareness of their fates compelled Lamar Keene to give up his practice of spiritualism:

> Looking ahead, if I stayed in mediumship, I saw only deepening gloom. All the mediums I've known or known about have had tragic endings.
>
> The Fox sisters, who started it all, wound up as alcoholic derelicts. William Slade, famed for his slate-writing tricks, died insane in a Michigan sanitarium. Margery the Medium lay on her deathbed a hopeless drunk. The celebrated Arthur Ford fought the battle of the bottle to the very end and lost. And the inimitable Mable Riffle, boss of Camp Chesterfield—well, when she died it was winter and freezing cold, and her body had to be held until a thaw for burial; the service was in the Cathedral at Chesterfield. Very few attended.
>
> Wherever I looked it was the same: mediums, at the end of a tawdry life, dying a tawdry death.[6]

Some people cite the story in 1 Samuel 28, where King Saul visited the medium at Endor and called up the deceased prophet Samuel, as evidence of genuine mediums. That is a dangerous conclusion. For one thing, the narrative never says that it actually was the ghost of Samuel. I don't believe that God would go against His specific command and do something He has condemned by bringing the spirit of Samuel back from the dead. In fact, if you study that passage carefully, you'll note that Saul never actually saw the form. The medium described what she saw, and everything "Samuel" spoke, she easily could have known. Another possible explanation is that a demon appeared, impersonating Samuel. Since God had cut off communication with Saul, I doubt that Samuel returned. In any case, this unique example in Scripture should not be used as evidence that contact with the dead is possible.

The Bible warns us not to attempt to contact the dead. Desire to communicate with a loved one is a real feeling, but comfort doesn't come from a medium. The prophet Isaiah wrote, "Why are you trying to find out the future by consulting witches and mediums? Don't listen to their whisperings and mutterings. Can the living find out the future from the dead? Why not ask your God?"[7] As a Christian, I can say with the apostle Paul that to be absent from the body is to be present with the Lord.[8] That is where our focus should be. Our hope is that when our loved ones die, if they are in Christ, they will go to be with God and we will join them at the time of our death.

Chapter Four

HOW PSYCHIC SURGEONS OPERATE

Jose Pedro de Freitas, a Brazilian peasant, became known throughout the world as "Arigo," the surgeon with the rusty knife. For more than twenty years, he saw some three hundred patients a day, five days a week. Each patient received a diagnosis, therapy and/or a written prescription. His normal method of treatment was to take a pocketknife, jab it into the body of the patient, twist it around, then reach in and pull out a growth or diseased tissue. Patients walked away without a scratch, and most of them claimed to be healed.

Stories are told of miraculous healers around the world. Each continent seems to have several so-called physicians with spiritual ability to perform in a matter of minutes what an ordinary doctor would consider complicated surgery. In 1982, Johanna Michaelsen wrote a book called *The Beautiful Side of Evil* about her experience with a psychic surgeon in Mexico. Ms. Michaelsen described several operations where she assisted Pachita, a woman who claimed to operate under the control of a male spirit doctor named Hermanito. One of her most vivid descriptions is of a back operation Pachita performed on a 72-year-old man from Los Angeles:

> One of the women knelt by Mr. Smith's head and began speaking softly to him. Hermanito had me pull up Mr. Smith's pajama top and fold his waistband down just enough to expose the lower back. I handed him a piece of alcohol-soaked cotton, which he rubbed briskly over the old man's back. Four large pieces of dry cotton were arranged in a square, leaving the spinal area where he would operate uncovered. He took the scissors in his hand and looked up at the intense faces in the room.
>
> "Lift your thoughts to God, my little ones—pray!"
>
> "Ask him if he is in pain." No he wasn't. Hermanito plunged one end of the scissors into his back. Mr. Smith groaned as it penetrated his skin. I saw the scissors disap-

pear into the back. I heard the flesh being cut. My hands on either side of the wound felt a warm thick liquid flow into the cotton. Mr. Smith groaned again . . . .

Hermanito pulled the scissors out. He took his knife, raised it in supplication and pushed it into Mr. Smith's back. I felt a fresh surge of warm liquid ooze up from the wound and over my fingers on the cotton. Hermanito cut away for several minutes, then reached in and pulled out what seemed to be an odd-shaped bone covered with blood and bits of red flesh.

"This is one of the vertebrae, little one. It is badly damaged." Hermanito then took another bone from a jar. As he did, I looked down into the dark gaping wound in Mr. Smith's back and felt a moment of panic.

"My God, how will this ever close and be whole again!" But then Hermanito turned and looked at me through those tight- shut eyes and I felt a deep peace take the place of fear. God was with us. Hermanito placed the bone inside the hole, then turned the knife upside down and with the blunt side hammered the bone into place. There was a dull squishing sound as it thudded against the wet raw flesh. Mr. Smith groaned. He was in pain.

. . . He cut out a second piece of bone inside the back and repeated the process.

"Are you watching closely, little daughter?" Hermanito asked me softly. I nodded affirmatively.

"This poor man," Hermanito said. "No wonder he has been in pain. There is a small tumor on the bone of his spine."

Again the knife went into the wound. Suddenly an incredible stench filled the room. Instinctively I lifted my hand up to my face, but Hermanito grabbed it and placed it back inside the wound. "Hold the tissue taut, little daughter. I must remove this tumor. It is cancerous." He cut something loose just above my fingers and pulled out a round, stringy mass of flesh about the size of a golfball which he then wrapped in cotton to be disposed of. Hermanito took a large piece of cotton which I handed him and swept the bloody cotton aside, passing his hand over the wound. It closed as he did so.[1]

How does one interpret such a spectacular story? Such an operation is a medical impossibility, yet this woman assisted in the operation and often was within inches of the incision, able to see everything. The question is even more difficult because the healer outwardly appears spiritual, urging spectators to pray and believe God for healing. And, in fact, many people *are* healed.

The problem is that most people are ill-equipped to evaluate such an operation. Even medical doctors can be deceived. Pachita, like other psychic surgeons I've observed, created a very effective illusion.

My first personal contact with psychic surgery was in Liberia, in 1968. Since then I have witnessed nearly 300 operations in Asia and Latin America. The best demonstrations by far were in the Philippines.

In the summer of 1973, David Aikman, a foreign correspondent for *Time* magazine, asked me to help him investigate several psychic surgeons in Baguio and Manila. I was eager to cooperate, since several Christians in the Philippines had expressed to me concern about these men, wondering if they were truly of God or satanic in origin. I was told that these surgeons could make a small incision in the body and reach through it to remove diseased tissue and organs. When they removed their hands, the skin closed, leaving no scar.

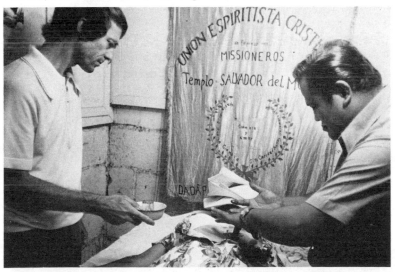

André Kole, in the Philippine Islands, investigates controversial psychic surgery phenomena.

During a three-day period, I witnessed more than fifty operations by seven different healers, five of whom were among the men most frequently mentioned in articles about spiritual healers. These men thought I was a news reporter, so they were very open and cooperative. They even asked me to assist in some operations, which gave me the best possible vantage point for studying their actions.

We first visited a plain, white, one-story building. Some two hundred people were lined up from the door and down the street, waiting to see the surgeon. The photographer and I were invited into the operating room. I felt anxious, not knowing what to expect, but the doctor, dressed in a colorful native shirt, immediately put me at ease and asked me to assist him. He was operating on a woman's back, removing a small cyst just below her shoulders.

The doctor began by holding my right index finger in the air and moving it in a short line about twelve inches above the cyst. As he did, a small incision, about an inch long, appeared. A numb feeling came over me when I saw that cut and realized it was genuine. I knew that if the incision closed and the woman walked out of the clinic without any scar, I truly would have witnessed something supernatural.

Quickly the doctor reached into the cut and removed a small mass of material that looked like gristle. Then he took a piece of cotton on a stick, dipped it in coconut oil, lit it and cauterized the cut; he did not heal the incision supernaturally. The whole operation took about three minutes.

It didn't take long to discover that the doctor used a very clever form of sleight of hand. The cut that my finger seemed to make actually was done with a small razor blade concealed in the healer's fingers. He concealed in his other hand the supposed diseased tissue, before apparently pulling it from the patient's body.

Strictly from the magician's point of view, apart from the moral and ethical issues, watching these healers was fascinating. They performed their fake operations using some of the most clever sleight of hand that I ever have seen. Their incredible dexterity immediately reminded me of the ability of Ben Chavez, a Philippine magician with nimble fingers and a quality of manual dexterity almost unequaled in the magic world.

Before his death, he trained some of today's best-known sleight-of-hand performers, and he taught me almost everything I know about prestidigitation. I never suspected how I would use this specialized knowledge in his country.

Most of these operations were performed on the abdominal area. Sometimes the surgeon made the operation more dramatic by making a small cut and covering it with a coin. Then he'd take a cotton ball soaked in coconut oil, lay it on the coin and light it. Next he'd cover it with a small glass, creating a suction that drew blood out into the glass. While the people watched that procedure, the healer secured a piece of animal tissue in his fingers. When he removed the glass and coin, he rubbed his fingers in the blood and made it appear that tissue was being removed from the incision.

Most of the time, the doctor did not actually cut the patient, yet his fingers appeared to reach through the skin and into the body, usually the stomach area. As I looked carefully, I saw that there was no opening in the skin, just a depressed area where the surgeon pushed, forming a small cup. By bending his fingers, he appeared to push them in much deeper than he did.

But what about the blood? The healers had put animal blood in a refrigerator to coagulate. Then they took some animal tissue, added a little of that blood, and wrapped cotton around it until it formed a ball. When it dried, it could be handled without getting messy. A bowl of water was always near the operating table. By quickly dipping this cotton in the water and gently massaging with it in the stomach area, blood appeared, and the tissue was available for quick removal. I later learned that some surgeons used a red dye made from betel nuts, rather than real blood, because it was less messy.

It was interesting to see the doctors' various procedures. Two men hid their loads, containing the tissue to be removed from the patient, underneath the table. Two others put theirs' in the open side of the pillow slip on which the patient was lying. Another got his load in the cotton his nurse gave to him. One man wore a loose shirt and hid his loads under the bottom hem.

Another popular operation involved removing an individual's eye. The healer began by poking around the patient's

45

eye, causing it to bulge from its socket. As he covered it with cotton, he appeared to take out the eye, but actually produced a cow or goat's eye. After washing it off and examining it, he supposedly replaced it. One doctor had used his animal eye so much that it had turned green.

I've viewed all these "operations," plus a couple of hundred more, in various parts of the world and on film, but I never have witnessed any evidence of supernatural healing ability. In every case, the surgeon used sleight of hand. Some people have said that the operations must be real because they have seen movies of them and could not see any tricks. Of course they could not see any tricks. If an average person—one not trained in sleight-of-hand techniques—could discover how the operations were done by watching the film, the healers would not have allowed the cameras. Several of my performances are on film and hundreds of copies are used around the world. People have slowed down the projector and even examined the film frame by frame, yet still could not tell how I did the tricks. I would not have put my effects on film if they could.

Some people see the accuracy of these doctors' diagnoses as evidence of their powers. Indeed they often do make correct diagnoses, which usually are educated guesses resulting from years of experience. They can "read" a person and size up a problem very quickly. When they aren't sure, they couch their guesses with very general statements that sound impressive but have little substance. If you kept a record of their diagnoses, you'd find that they miss at least as many as they hit.

Soon after my experience in the Philippines, I was asked to be an expert witness for the Federal Trade Commission in a case against several travel agencies in the Pacific Northwest. The agencies were promoting special tours to these healers in the Philippines. Unfortunately some people never made it home, and others died soon after they returned, experiencing no benefits from their treatments.

That disturbed me the most about these men. I saw people who needed genuine medical attention come to these psychic surgeons. One young boy had burned his nose and it was swollen to the size of a tennis ball. Another patient had his appendix "removed" three times, and finally a regular doctor removed it surgically.

Many of these healers appeared to be very sincere. Some felt they were helping people believe in God; they prayed over the patients and read from the Bible. But they also told people that if they didn't have enough faith, they wouldn't be healed. That gave the doctors a good excuse when a person wasn't healed—it wasn't his fault but the patient's. He would have been healed if only he'd had more faith.

After viewing the operations, I interviewed a number of the patients, asking them if they were helped. Many answered,"I think so" or "I hope so." Yet, as I went down the line of people waiting to see the healer, I saw many returning with the same problems they had brought in previous weeks. Some had the same operation performed on them week after week.

Others were genuinely helped and even cured by these surgeries. The percentage of people cured, however, is much lower than articles written about the subject lead one to believe. And any healings do not result from the operations, which are fake, but from the operations' psychological effect on people who believe they are real.

One of the best studies on this phenomenon is by William A. Nolen, M.D. In his book, *Healings: A Doctor in Search of a Miracle,* Nolen examined hundreds of volumes and visited several of the best-known faith healers, including several Filipino psychic surgeons, looking for "adequately documented examples of cures that could not reasonably be explained except in terms of miraculous powers." He could not find one such case.[2]

In the final chapters of his book, Nolen describes the healing process, which he concludes is a mystery: " . . . we doctors don't do the healing; the body does. And even though, by examining specimens of tissue in various stages of healing, we know something of how healing occurs, we don't as yet have any idea how to control it. We put things back together; the body—God, if you prefer—heals."[3]

So how are these people healed? Nolen writes: "It is possible that 'healers,' by their machinations, their rituals, their sheer charisma, stimulate patients so that they heal more rapidly than they otherwise might; charismatic doctors do the same. In all probability, this is why doctors who have warm rapport with their patients seem to get better results than doctors who treat their patients briskly and impersonally."[4]

The whole point of his book is that certain illnesses successfully lend themselves to treatment of this type. Others will naturally, over the course of time, heal without any outside help. At least half of all illnesses fall into these two categories, so any psychic healer automatically should have a success rate of at least 50 percent.

Nolen explains that the problem is with organic diseases, such as heart attacks, infections, gallstones, hernias, slipped discs, cancers of all kinds, broken bones, congenital deformities, and many others. He writes:

> These are the diseases that healers, even the most charismatic, cannot cure. When they attempt to do so—and they all fall into this trap, since they know and care nothing of the differences between functional and organic diseases—they tread on very dangerous ground. When healers treat serious organic diseases they are responsible for untold anguish and unhappiness; this happens because they keep patients away from possibly effective and lifesaving help. The healers become killers.
>
> Search the literature, as I have, and you will find no documented cures by healers of gallstones, heart disease, cancer or any other serious organic disease. Certainly, you'll find patients temporarily relieved of their upset stomachs, their chest pains, their breathing problems; and you will find healers, and believers, who will interpret this interruption of symptoms as evidence that the disease is cured. But when you track the patient down and find out what happened later, you always find the "cure" to have been purely symptomatic and transient. The underlying disease remains.[5]

Several doctors actually have endorsed these psychic healers while recognizing the absurdity of the operations. They are taken in because they are not trained in the field of deception. It would take too much time and space to describe all the variations and techniques these healers use, but the average person could never detect their trickery. So many people are deceived because they try to explain the operations in terms of science, psychology, theology or medicine. That actually assists the healers by further drawing attention from their sleight of hand.

At the start of this chapter, I related a very dramatic case of psychic surgery. Soon after this operation, Johanna Michaelson began to seriously question her involvement with this medium. She wondered why she was not progressing in her own ability to become a full-trance medium. She witnessed some exciting successes by Pachita-Hermanito, but also some disillusioning setbacks. The telling blow was the death of a childhood friend just four months after his "operation."

Yet the operations seem so real. I have found that the most dramatic operations often are performed on American patients. Usually a psychic surgeon will not go to a lot of trouble unless he wants to especially impress the patient, observer or both. Ms. Michaelson mentioned that Pachita sometimes added realism with human parts she secured from a friend at a morgue.

Tony Agpaoa, probably the best known Filipino surgeon, did the same thing. He also stretched a thin piece of goat intestine over the patient before making an incision. Cutting through it created the illusion of cutting the skin and caused a snapping sound. Then he reached down into the incision and pulled out what he claimed was a diseased organ, such as an appendix, tumor or a damaged vertebra. He disposed of the extra piece of skin in a bucket below the table, and left no trace of an incision on the patient, since no cut was made.

Because of my experience, I am very skeptical of reports about miraculous healing. People describe all sorts of spectacular feats that the healers could not possibly have done. Most operations are relatively minor, and exaggerated reports about cancer being cured, ruptured disks being repaired and gallstones disappearing simply can't be substantiated.

For years during my show I cut my wife in half, then apparently divided the two parts of her body and walked through the center. I would have her move her head on one side of the stage, and move her feet on the other side of the stage. People were constantly baffled by the effect. They didn't know how I did it, but they knew that it must be a trick because I called myself a magician and I performed it on a stage.

But suppose I called myself a surgeon and performed the same procedure in an operating room, smearing some blood and using medical terms in a serious manner. If I claimed to correct an internal problem while she was divided, and even produced some tissue for effect, many would think they were witnessing something supernatural. It certainly would be far more dramatic than anything these psychic healers produce. But it would be just as fraudulent.

A very important element in this study is the question of faith. The healers tell their patients that if they have enough faith, they will be healed. If the surgery was genuine, however, it wouldn't matter if the patient believed or not. A successful appendectomy depends on the surgeon's skill, not the patient's faith. Yet some people are healed after visiting psychic healers. I cannot say whether or not God healed them, or if it released psychosomatic symptoms. (I will further examine faith healing and divine healing in chapter 14.) But they definitely were not healed by the operation, which was a trick. Jesus warned of the consequences of falsely claiming supernatural power. He said, "Not all who sound religious are really godly people. They may refer to Me as 'Lord,' but still won't get to heaven. For the decisive question is whether they obey My Father in heaven. At the judgment many will tell Me, 'Lord, Lord, we told others about You and used Your name to cast out demons and to do many other great miracles.' But I will reply, 'You have never been Mine. Go away, for your deeds are evil.' "[6]

Chapter Five

HOW POWERFUL IS THE MIND?

In the early 1970s, a handsome young man with a mop of dark wavy hair burst into the public consciousness. On television shows and in laboratory experiments, the Israeli bent metal objects such as spoons and keys, fixed watches, recreated drawings without seeing them, predicted the roll of a die in a box, and altered the direction of a compass—all through only the use of his mind, or so he claimed. The perpetrator of those feats was Uri Geller, and many still refer to him as a prime example of the human mind's potential power.

For years extrasensory perception, "ESP," has fascinated people. But what is ESP? Dr. Joseph Banks Rhine, for years head of the parapsychology laboratory at Duke University, originated the term, which is defined as the ability to perceive or act outside the realm of the five senses.

Generally, this is broken down into four manifestations. *Clairvoyance*, sometimes called second sight, is the ability to identify objects or events without using the five senses. Someone might demonstrate it by reading or driving while blindfolded, or describing an object or location he has never seen. The second, *telepathy*, or mind reading, is communication between two minds by means other than normal sensory channels. *Precognition*, also called divination or premonition, is knowledge of a future event or state that cannot be inferred from present information. Finally, *psychokinesis* (often referred to as PK, or sometimes telekinesis) is the mind's ability to influence physical objects without using any physical energy or instrumentation.

The question is, do any or all of these elements of ESP (or psi, as it often is called) actually exist? Many people feel that most or all humans have latent ESP potential. They refer to numerous experiments, and particularly to a handful of well-publicized psychic superstars.

Perhaps the most commonly cited example is Uri Geller, who supposedly has demonstrated all four elements of ESP. Geller received much publicity after his powers were tested at the Stanford Research Institute (SRI) in Palo Alto by Doctors Russell Targ and Harold Puthoff.

Targ and Puthoff published their findings in a very controversial article in *Nature* magazine, a highly respected scientific journal. They wrote that the results of their experiments suggest "The existence of one or more perceptual modalities through which individuals obtain information about their environment, although this information is not presented to any known sense."[1]

They reported on three experiments. First Geller was asked to reproduce simple line drawings, called targets, "while separated from both the target material and anyone knowledgeable of the material." Results of the thirteen separate drawing experiments were mixed. Geller did duplicate one of the pictures, a cluster of twenty-two grapes. He also was reasonably close on four of the other twelve drawings. On three targets, he "got no clear impression"[2] and refused to submit drawings.

A second series of experiments involved a hundred target pictures sealed in envelopes and randomly divided into groups of twenty. Geller was asked to associate any envelope with a drawing he made. He expressed "dissatisfaction with the existence of such a large target pool" and refused to associate any of his drawings with specific envelopes. On each of the three days, two of his drawings "could reasonably be associated with two of the daily targets." But the authors concluded, "The drawings resulting from this experiment do not depart significantly from what would be expected by chance."[3]

The third experiment yielded the most spectacular results. After a die was shaken in an enclosed steel box, Geller was asked to identify its uppermost face. In ten tries, Geller passed twice and gave the correct response the other eight times. The authors concluded that the probability of this occurring by chance was approximately one in one million.

Regarding Geller's metal bending ability, the authors declined comment, saying that they were not able to observe it under sufficiently controlled circumstances to support his claim of psychokinesis.

For all the publicity generated by the experiments, the results were not particularly impressive. In fact the editors of *Nature* expressed concern over the article:

> All the referees felt that the details given of various safeguards and precautions introduced against the possibility of conscious or unconscious fraud on the part of one or other of the subjects were "uncomfortably vague"This in itself might be sufficient to raise doubt that the experiments have demonstrated the existence of a new channel of communication which does not involve the use of the senses.[4]

Author-researcher Martin Gardner examined Geller's most sensational experiment, where he correctly called the roll of a die in a steel box. He pointed out that Puthoff and Targ "describe the die test with a brevity that seems inappropriate for so extraordinary a claim. We are not told who shook the box, where or when the test was made, who observed the trials, how long Geller took to make each guess, whether he was allowed to touch the box, whether there were earlier or later die-box tests with Uri, or whether the experiment was visually recorded."[5]

Gardner correctly concluded that Geller could have cheated in many ways. The only way to rule out the possibility of trickery would have been to have a knowledgeable magician present, or to see a videotape of all the attempts. "In the absence of such controls for guarding against deception by a known charlatan the die test was far too casual and slipshod to deserve being included in a technical paper for a journal as reputable as *Nature*," Gardner concluded.[6]

I believe that Gardner and the editors of *Nature* were right to express concern. What most people do not realize about Uri Geller—what he has tried to suppress in his publicity—is that he studied and practiced magic as a youth in Israel. But he quickly realized that he attracted a far greater following by claiming paranormal powers than he did as a conjurer. In fact, most of what he does would be rather insignificant coming from a magician.

Geller also is a clever opportunist. Friends of mine who have observed him say he is a master at taking advantage of a situation. At a table full of silverware and keys, he may bend one, but he rarely announces what he will do, so people don't know what to expect. He has the audience under his control. In a controlled setting, when asked to bend one specific object without handling it, his powers mysteriously disappear.

Persi Diaconis, a professor of statistics at Stanford University, tells a story that demonstrates Geller's methods. Diaconis drove Geller to the airport after he'd appeared at Stanford. While waiting for his flight, the psychic expressed disappointment that the professor remained a skeptic, and he offered to provide conclusive proof of his powers. He then asked Diaconis to reach into his coat pocket, grab his keys and concentrate on a key that could be bent. The professor says, "I opened my hand and the key I was thinking of was bent. For about five minutes I was as badly fooled as I've ever been in my life."

Diaconis solved the mystery by reviewing the trip to the airport. Geller had insisted on sitting in the back seat, where Diaconis' coat lay. At the airport parking lot, Geller had insisted that he bring the coat "in case it gets too cool." The key ring contained four keys, only one of which could be bent easily. When he further examined his coat, he discovered an envelope turned inside out, and each of his pens' tops bent and twisted. Geller apparently had prepared several "proofs" of his powers.

A good friend of mine, Ray Hyman, professor of psychology at the University of Oregon, observed Geller firsthand during a portion of the SRI experiments. We talked about it one evening after I did a show on his campus. When I expressed my opinion that Geller seemed almost satanically cunning—that his cleverness seemed to come from another source—Dr. Hyman responded by characterizing Geller as a "pathological liar," a person who has "no twinge of conscience." He illustrated his point: "Geller spent the whole morning doing what I consider just blatant trickery. And now I was having lunch with him and I said, 'Look Geller, I know you made your living in Israel working nightclubs and doing entertaining. Have you ever, in your career, used trickery at all?' He looked at me and put his hand over his heart. Tears welled up in his eyes. 'Ray, how could you even ask such a question of me? If I ever cheated even once, how could I live with myself?' At that moment I felt like a heel, even though I knew the guy was cheating right and left."

That's just another example of the charm and personality of Geller. When confronted by skeptics, rather than substantiate his claims, he often plays the role of a misunderstood genius and puts his opponents on the defensive.

Hyman also observed that Geller was very quick to pick up sensory clues from people. He learned what people expected from him as a psychic, and he didn't disappoint them. In a casual conversation, one SRI scientist said that psychics seemed to be very sensitive to electronic equipment. An hour later Geller balked at an experiment because a video machine was giving off "bad vibes." "Several times I would ask him a question," Hyman told me, "and before he could answer, one of the scientists would butt in and give the answer. Sure enough, when the subject came up again, Geller would rephrase what the scientist had said earlier."

All of this illustrates a point that I often make in my programs. Even the most intelligent people can be deceived when presented with a phenomenon—no matter how ridiculous—in a serious manner, in an atmosphere where honesty is taken for granted. The sad fact is that scientists may be the most ill-equipped to detect fraud. They will go to elaborate lengths to eliminate any possible form of sensory input in ESP experiments, but if they miss even one, then that avenue must be examined before their conclusions can be verified.

Hyman is in a unique position to verify this point because as a youth he became an accomplished magician and mentalist. The money he made from his mind-reading act helped put him through school. After earning a Ph.D. in psychology at Johns Hopkins University, he served as a professor at Harvard before moving to Oregon. He is one of the leading international experts in the investigation of the paranormal.

"It is fairly easy to fool a scientist," Hyman says, "because he thinks very logically. Scientists can cope with nature because nature doesn't change the rules. But an alleged psychic changes the rules. He takes advantage of the way you think and leads you down his path of deception. That's why children are much harder to fool—they aren't as well conditioned."

Project Alpha confirmed that. In 1979 Washington University in St. Louis, Missouri, was awarded a $500,000 grant to form a laboratory for psychical research. James Randi arranged for two teenage magicians, Steve Shaw and Michael Edwards, to apply to the lab as candidates for a study on psychokinetic metal-bending by children. From among 300 applicants, they were the only two subjects chosen.

The scientists never suspected that they were set up, and the two boys performed all sorts of "amazing" feats in the lab. "There is no question that the lab personnel believed that Mike and Steve were actually psychic," wrote Randi after he and the two subjects exposed the project two years later. "It was this belief that made the deception exceedingly easy, and it was clear that, had the two entered the arena as conjurors, they could never have gotten away with all they did."[7]

This leads me to state two guidelines for anyone reading about or investigating paranormal powers. When investigating a potential case of ESP, assume every other possible explanation first. *The conclusion of ESP can be made only after every other possible natural explanation has been examined and eliminated.*

For most people, eliminating all the options is nearly impossible, as many methods are used to obtain information from a person without his knowledge. One is called cold reading, or unconscious sensory cueing. It is the ability to learn all sorts of information about a person from body language and facial expressions. It's great psychology, but a person using it may appear to read minds. We will discuss cold reading more in the next chapter.

Uri Geller often complains that he can't perform when a skeptic is in the room. (And especially if that skeptic is a magician!) He's using good showmanship, and protecting himself when controls become too tight. People usually are very sympathetic to that argument because they want to believe. But if someone really had psychic powers, we could reasonably expect him to demonstrate them under tightly controlled conditions. If nothing else, the monetary rewards would be fantastic. (Such a person could make a financial killing in a place like Las Vegas.)

A second guideline is: *Be wary of statistics.* Geller's chances of calling eight rolls of a die without a miss was one in a million. That seems most impressive, but all it tells you is that it didn't happen by accident. In and of itself, that doesn't prove the existence of ESP.

Persi Diaconis wrote about this in *Science* magazine. After reviewing several psi (parapsychology) experiments, he stated, "Most often these tests are 'highly statistically significant.' This only implies that the results are improbable under simple chance models. In complex, badly controlled experiments simple chance models cannot be seriously considered as tenable explanations; hence rejection of such models is not of particular interest."[8]

Diaconis went on to examine how statistical data can be drastically skewed if just one or two details of an experiment are altered; for example, if a subject receives unconscious sensory cues. "There always seem to be many loopholes and loose ends," he says in his conclusion. "The same mistakes are made again and again."[9]

Why are people so fascinated with ESP? I think author Dave Hunt (whose eight books include *Cult Explosion* and *Peace, Prosperity and the Coming Holocaust*) isolated the real issue when he said, "I believe that the ultimate purpose, the ultimate goal, of psychic power is to validate Satan's lie—the lie that man is God. Unless humanity can manifest these powers, they can't really validate what Satan has promised . . . .As to the various manifestations of psi, you could categorize them as attempts to mimic the attributes of God, because they try to appropriate the omnipotence, omniscience and omnipresence of God. This is basically the *function* of psychic phenomena, theologically speaking."[10]

For several years, transcendental meditation was the rage among young people. But when participation dropped off, the movement, under the leadership of Maharishi Mahesh Yogi, came up with the idea of teaching students to levitate—for a substantial fee. This seems to be an ultimate dream of those who wish to use mind power. The Maharishi claimed that people could levitate through a purified, altered state of consciousness, and practice. Thousands of students enrolled, paying between $3,000 and $5,000 each for the privilege of bouncing up and down. No one from the program, however, could publicly demonstrate the ability to levitate.

One of the highlights of my show is the self-levitation illusion in which I appear to rise and float about five feet above the stage. As you can see from the photo, it is a most effective illusion. It baffles audiences, but it is accomplished entirely by natural methods. As I have said, I have no supernatural powers whatsoever.

Since I began practicing magic, I have performed eleven different forms of levitation. In my travels around the world, including five tours of India, I have attempted to find just one genuine demonstration of levitation. I have not succeeded. I feel confident that if someone had that ability, I would learn about it quickly through my worldwide network of magician-friends.

One thing I haven't addressed in this discussion about mind power is the occasional unexplainable premonitions that many have experienced. Almost all of us know a friend or relative who has had a dramatic premonition for no apparently logical reason. Is ESP a possible explanation?

I know of two such experiences in my family. One time my parents were in a movie theater when my mother sensed that my brother was in trouble and she began to cry. Later we found out that he was in an accident at that very moment, but he

One of eleven different forms of levitation that André has performed.

wasn't seriously hurt.

Another case involved my brother-in-law. He was driving a car when he suddenly had a tremendous impression that his father had died. He had to pull off the road because he was so emotionally upset. When they arrived home, a call informed him that his father had died at the exact moment the feeling had come over him.

Many cases like this are recorded. They are real and difficult to explain. But they don't prove the existence of ESP because they are only one-time, isolated events. No one has demonstrated such power in a regular, everyday manner.

Luis Alvarez of the University of California at Berkeley has one statistical explanation. Using a complex statistical analysis he concludes that events such as I described should occur about ten times per day around the United States. "With such a large sample to draw from, it is not surprising that some exceedingly astonishing coincidences are reported in the parapsychological literature as proof of extrasensory perception in one form or another."[11]

Psychologists have an even better explanation. "My brother was killed in World War II and my mother had a dream about it the night before it happened," Ray Hyman says. "Both my mother and sister believe it was a prophetic dream, but I see nothing miraculous about it. All three of us had that dream many times. They just don't remember the others because nothing happened to make them come true.

"The current theory of memory is that you tend to remember those things that you can connect to something meaningful. Let's say you periodically have fleeting thoughts of Uncle Moe, but they come and go and you forget them. Then one day you happen to think of Uncle Moe and he calls that evening. You say to yourself, 'I haven't thought about Uncle Moe for years.' You probably thought of Uncle Moe many times, but nothing happened to make those thoughts memorable."

I enjoy performing an illusion in which my eyes are covered by two half-dollars, taped shut and covered with a blindfold. Then I invite members of the audience to test me. Without touching anything, I identify the colors of several scarves, identify objects such as wallets and combs, and read words they wrote on 3" by 5" cards.

Sound impressive? Would you believe I have the power of ESP? I want to assure you that I have no such power. Over the years, I practiced sometimes twelve to sixteen hours a day with cards to master the art of finger manipulation. Often my finger tips were raw from the hours of practice, however, they never became so sensitive that I could identify objects, tell colors, or accomplish any of the other amazing feats I apparently do with my finger tips. I certainly do not have ESP, and I would strongly question anyone who claims that he does.

Chapter Six

PREDICTING THE FUTURE

* New York City, Albany and Boston soon will be destroyed.[1]
* The Civil War will be the start of a global conflict.[2]
* The moon is inhabited by a people of uniform size, about six feet in height.[3]
* In a few years, the people of the United States will be destroyed by pestilence, hail, famine and earthquake.[4]

These prophecies were delivered between 1832 and 1837. They sound crazy now, yet the man who proclaimed them was a respected religious leader, whose followers now number in the millions. He is just one example of why we must be wary of modern-day prophets.

Millions of people spend their money in belief or hope that they can satisfy their curiosity about the future. They use astrology, palm reading and modern-day seers like Jeane Dixon to help them plan their lives. But are modern-day prognosticators legitimate? Can anyone predict the future?

I apply four basic tests whenever people claim to have psychic ability to predict future events: (1) How specific are their predictions? (2) What percentage of their forecasts are accurate? (3) Do their lives back up their claims? (4) What is the source (or claimed source) of their information?

Let's look at these questions in more detail. First: *How specific are their predictions?*

Psychic superstar Jeane Dixon is perhaps best known for predicting the assassination of President John Kennedy. *Parade Magazine* (May 13, 1956) reported, "As to the 1960 election, Mrs. Dixon thinks it will be dominated by labor and won by a Democrat. But he will be assassinated or die in office, though not necessarily in his first term."

This is a classic example of vagueness that can, in retrospect, look like an accurate hit. Mrs. Dixon predicted a Democrat would win—her chances of being right were 50-50. She didn't say who. And it wasn't a huge risk to predict that the president would die in office. Already three had done so in the twentieth century, and observers saw a cycle: the president elected every 20 years from the year 1840 either had been assassinated or had died while in office. Mrs. Dixon wasn't willing to state how the president would die, whether or not it would be an assassination, or even approximately when it would take place. If the president served two terms, she conceivably had eight years for her prophecy to be fulfilled. So her most spectacular forecast really wasn't that impressive.

But often that is how modern prophets work. Right now I can make some "prophecies" similar to that of many seers. I can tell you with a high degree of confidence that within the next 12 months:

  * A major earthquake will take place, killing more than a hundred people.
  * A major world figure will die in office.
  * A major technological breakthrough will amaze the world and change our lives.

It doesn't take a prophet to make these kinds of predictions. It only takes a good observer, someone aware of what is happening around him in the world.

One of the post popular prophets over the last few centuries was the sixteenth century seer Nostradamus. At age fifty, he began composing vague quatrains (four-line verses) which he said were predictions. He divided the more than nine hundred verses into groups of one hundred, with each grouping representing a century. The prophecies contained elaborate symbolism and codes that Nostradamus admitted could not possibly be understood until after the events they predicted. That has led to several interesting interpretations over the years. For example, in World War II, the Allied forces and the Germans used the same verse to prove opposite conclusions. A. Voldben, in his book *After Nostradamus* writes about the prophet he praises:

> The quatrains are strewn about without any order in such a way that even if the beginning were found it would not be possible to continue them in the right order. They are usually vague, involved in the confused langue of

sybilline oracles, some literal and some symbolic. So much so that in the confusion between literal and symbolic, one is left hardly understanding anything at all! If some are easy to understand, others are incomprehensible. He writes in the French of his day, mixed with Latin words with others made up by him and his own anagrams.[5]

It makes you wonder why people still diligently study his work. Yet Nostradamus is extremely popular, especially on university campuses.

My second question logically follows from the first: *What percentage of the prophet's predictions are accurate?*

In promoting their forecasts, today's prophets proudly recall their hits, while hoping that people will forget or ignore their misses. The public generally complies. When specific, verifiable predictions are made, it's relatively simple to go back and check the record. F. K. Donnelly, associate professor of history at the University of New Brunswick in Canada, reviewed the predictions that twenty-one psychics made in *The People's Almanac,* 1975 edition. The seers included Malcolm Bessent, David Bubar, Jeane Dixon, Irene Hughes and many other well-known psychics. Donnelly evaluated their predictions from the time they were made through 1981:

> Out of the total of 72 predictions, 66 (or 92 percent) were dead wrong. Among the favorites in this category were those that China would go to war with the United States (predicted 4 times) and that New York City would soon be underwater (predicted 3 times). My favorite inept prognostication comes from the Berkeley Psychic Institute, which predicted a war between Greenland and the Soviet Union over fish. Since nuclear weapons were to be used, this war was to be very sensibly fought in Labrador in May 1977.[6]

Of the six predictions that were not wrong, two were only partially right or vague. Two others were not exactly graphic evidence of psychic power: Russia and the United States would "remain as leading world powers," and there would be no world wars between 1975 and 1980. Donnelly concludes, "Even if we were to accept that four (or 6 percent) of the 72 predictions were correct . . . a further problem remains. Since we do not know which of the 72 predictions will fall into the six-percent

63

category, then of what use is this? Who among us would take the advice of a tipster with a track record of being wrong more than nine times out of ten?"[7]

It's easy to evaluate Jeane Dixon's track record. Here are just a few of her prophecies that haven't come true:

1) Russia would be the first nation to put men on the moon.
2) World War III would begin in 1954.
3) The Vietnam war would end in 1966. (It didn't end until 1975.)
4) On October 19, 1968, she predicted Jacqueline Kennedy was not thinking of marriage. The next day Mrs. Kennedy married Aristotle Onassis.
5) In 1970, she predicted Castro would be overthrown from Cuba and would have to leave the island.[8]

These are just a handful of many examples. The problem is, people only remember the successes. When you compare Mrs. Dixon's hits with her misses, you find that her percentage of accuracy is most unimpressive.

I opened this chapter with four prophecies made by Joseph Smith, founder of the Mormon church. Smith claimed to be a prophet of God, and in the course of eighteen years he made sixty-four specific prophecies. Only six of them were fulfilled. Many of his proclamations dealt with the future of his church. For example, in August of 1831 he stated that God had told him, "The faithful among you shall be preserved and rejoice together in the land of Missouri."[9] In September of 1832, he stated that the city of Independence would become the "New Jerusalem . . . even the place of the temple, which temple shall be reared in this generation."[10] Six years later the Mormons were driven out of Independence. No temple was built there. Eventually they were drive from Missouri and settled in Utah.

I could cite many other prophecies. Smith predicted the return of Jesus Christ to earth by the year 1890. He said Indians converted to Mormonism would turn white. He proclaimed that the United States would be utterly destroyed if there was not redress for the wrongs committed against Mormons in Missouri. None of these were fulfilled.

Third, I think it is important *to evaluate the lives of the persons making psychic claims.* The most revealing article I've found about Jeane Dixon was out of the *National Observer* (reprinted by *The Christian Reader*). The author, Daniel St. Albin Greene, spent weeks investigating her subject. "What gradually emerged," she wrote, "was a portrait of neither saint nor charlatan, but of a beguiling enigma whose real identity has been absorbed by the myth she herself created."[11]

Ms. Greene examined the chapters in Jeane Dixon's life that she has tried to suppress. It turns out that legend, not reality, made Mrs. Dixon's career. And it is a legend of her own making. "All the public knows about Jeane Dixon is what she has said."[12]

The article examined the claim that Mrs. Dixon has never used her "God-given gifts" for personal profit. In fact, her book royalties and revenue from her syndicated columns were paid to a company Mrs. Dixon and her husband owned. Sponsors of her speeches donated money to a charitable foundation run by her. The foundation, Children to Children, actually had distributed less than 19 percent of its income.

Most of the information about Mrs. Dixon's background is found in *A Gift of Prophecy: The Phenomenal Jeane Dixon* by Ruth Montgomery. A detailed check of records revealed that much of her earlier biographical material was fiction. A total of fourteen years, including a former marriage, had disappeared from her past.

> If nothing else, the purged 14 years constitute a credibility gap that undermines the whole foundation of the Jeane Dixon story as told my Mrs. Dixon. Rereading the biography of her pre-Washington period in the new time frame, one must constantly choose among three possibilities: each incident that Mrs. Dixon says took place when she was a child prodigy in California either (1) actually occurred many years earlier in the Midwest; (2) happened when she was in her 20s or 30s; or (3) never happened at all.[13]

Such revelations severely limit her credibility. The same could be said about Joseph Smith. For the most part, the Mormons are very sincere, nice people, but the Mormon church stands or falls on the reputation of this one man.

A careful examination of Smith's life reveals many disturbing facts. Perhaps most damaging are the various versions of his first vision, in which he says God the Father (and/or Jesus Christ, an angel, or a pillar of light, depending on the version) appeared to him when he was sixteen years old (later amended to when he was fourteen years old). In this version, Smith was told that all churches were wrong, and that "all their creeds are an abomination in His sight."

Fawn Brodie states in the supplement of her meticulously researched book, *No Man Knows My History: The Life of Joseph Smith the Mormon Prophet.*

> One of the major original premises of this biography was that Joseph Smith's assumption of the role of a religious prophet was an evolutionary process, that he began as a bucolic scryer, using the primitive techniques of the folklore of magic common to his area, most of which he discarded as he evolved into a preacher-prophet. There seemed to be good evidence that when he chose to write of this evolution in his *History of the Church* he distorted the past in the interest of promoting his public image as a gifted young prophet with a substantial and growing following. There was evidence even to stimulate doubt of the authenticity of the "first vision," which Joseph Smith declared in his official history had occurred in 1820 when he was fourteen.[14]

Numerous points darken this man's integrity. The 1835 edition of *Doctrine & Covenants* condemned fornication and polygamy and admonished, "One man should have one wife; and one woman but one husband; except that in the event of death when either is at liberty to marry again." Those words became a problem for Joseph Smith as he had affairs with more and more women. Finally, he received a "new revelation" in 1843 giving God's blessing on plural marriages. The earlier command simply disappeared, without explanation, from later editions of *Doctrine & Covenants.* As best as Brodie can determine, Smith had forty-eight wives when he died in 1844.[15]

There are also many reasons to doubt the *Book of Mormon.* Joseph Smith said of this book, the keystone of his religion, that it "was the most correct of any book on earth."[16] Yet since its first printing in 1830, there have been 3,913 changes, as documented by Jerald and Sandra Tanner who marked all of the changes on a photo reprint of the original edition.

Besides that, archeology cannot verify the *Book of Mormon*, whereas the Bible is one of the best documented books of history.

Most of the mountains, rivers, cities and regions named in the Bible have been identified by archeological scholars. But Josh McDowell and Don Stewart have summarized the problem with the *Book of Mormon*:

1. No *Book of Mormon* cities have been located.
2. No *Book of Mormon* names have been found in New World inscriptions.
3. No genuine inscriptions have been found in Hebrew in America.
4. No genuine inscriptions have been found in America in Egyptian or anything similar to Egyptian, which could correspond to Joseph Smith's "reformed Egyptian."
5. No ancient copies of *Book of Mormon* scriptures have been found.
6. No ancient inscriptions of any kind in America which indicate that the ancient inhabitants had Hebrew or Christian beliefs have been found.
7. No mention of *Book of Mormon* persons, nations, or places have been found.[17]

Why be concerned with such details? Are they really that important? I believe that a person who claims to be a prophet creates for himself a high standard. By stating that he has divine revelations, he opens himself to scrutiny to see if his life supports his claims. J. Edward Decker, a former priest in the Mormon church, writes, "A lie is a lie is a lie, and when it comes out of the mouth of a man proclaimed to be a prophet of God, that man is sent not of God, neither has God commanded him."[18]

The final question is: *What is the source of the prophet's information?*

A favorite trick among magicians is to make a prediction of future news headlines—the winner of an election, the World Series champion, a winning lottery number—and seal it inside an envelope. Then the envelope is locked inside a safe. The more secure it appears, the better. It is best to have 24-hour security to verify that no one tampers with that safe. Of course, after the result is known, the envelope is opened amidst great fanfare to reveal that the magician had correctly predicted the event.

Many books explain various methods to accomplish this

trick. Elaborate paraphernalia, some costing thousands of dollars, can help successfully create this illusion. Some inexpensive methods also do the trick, such as one I used one night during my show. I correctly predicted who would shoot J.R. of "Dallas" two hours before it was due to be aired on local television. My audience was amazed, as this was one of television's best-kept secrets. CBS had filmed several versions, so even the cast didn't know who the culprit was. But my audience didn't know that backstage I had an open phone line to a friend on the East Coast. Of course, East Coast viewers would learn the answer three hours earlier than those in the West, where I was performing. Mystery solved!

One of the most blatant frauds was a tape of blond psychic Tamara Rand predicting the attempted assassination of President Reagan nearly three months ahead of the event. The tape was shown on a Los Angeles station and then repeated on NBC's "Today Show" and ABC's "Good Morning America." Several newspapers published an Associated Press story about it before one of the cameramen who had filmed Ms. Rand revealed the truth. The tape actually had been made two days after the assassination attempt. Before she finally confessed, Ms. Rand tried to explain that she merely had been asked to "rearticulate" her prophecy in front of cameras because her words were not clear on the earlier tape.[19]

Some psychics claim that they have a God-given gift. Jeane Dixon always has made this claim. If indeed she has a gift from God, then God must make an awful lot of mistakes! The facts are conclusive that she has no gift of God. The Bible makes it clear that one evidence of a genuine prophet is that he *never* makes a wrong prediction. "And you may say in your heart, 'How shall we know the word which the Lord has spoken?' When a prophet speaks in the name of the Lord, if the thing does not come about or come true, that is the thing which the Lord has not spoken. The prophet has spoken it presumptuously; you shall not be afraid of him."[20]

Many others have expressed their belief that Jeane Dixon is demon-possessed. If that is true, then she is possessed by a dumb bunch of demons.

Another primary tool of the fortune-telling trade is called cold reading. It is used primarily by palm readers and those who use a crystal ball, tarot cards or tea leaves. Magicians also use it in stage shows to demonstrate "mind reading" skills.

Cold reading is a combination of things, but essentially the reader gives back information that the client unknowingly has given him. He starts with a pre-prepared character assessment that is general enough to encompass approximately 85 percent of the population. The reader says things like, "You have many acquaintances but few close friends....People frequently call on you for advice ... You have a tendency to worry at times ... You tend to put off jobs that must be done but that don't interest you. ...."

Ray Hyman explains the next step:

> The cold reader basically relies on a good memory and acute observation. The client is carefully studied. The clothing—for example, style, neatness, cost, age—provides a host of cues for helping the reader make shrewd guesses about socioeconomic level, conservatism or extroversion, and other characteristics. The client's physical features—weight, posture, looks, eyes, and hands provide further cues. The hands are especially revealing to the good reader. The manner of speech, use of grammar, gestures, and eye contact are also good sources. To the good reader the huge amount of information coming from an initial sizing-up of the client greatly narrows the possible categories into which he classifies clients.[21]

After his stock spiel, the cold reader begins to address the client's problems and watches the reaction to determine whether or not he's on the right track. He is also a good listener and many times takes what he has heard and later rephrases it to sound like a fresh revelation. Fortune tellers have learned that most clients already have decided what they want to do and simply want support to carry out their decision. General and ambiguous statements can be taken to mean whatever the client wants them to mean. Later the predictions seem more accurate than they really were.

Another area of prophecy is astrology. After my shows I frequently am asked my opinion of it. Three of my suggested questions again apply: How specific are the predictions? What percentage is accurate? What is the source of information?

Immediately we can discount the daily horoscopes in the newspapers. The statements are so general that true astrologers don't take them seriously. "Be careful on the highway . . . .Make sure you don't spend too much on pleasure and then later regret it . . . .You may not like what a fellow worker is doing . . . .One who has problems expects your aid . . . ." and so on. These statements could apply to anyone and don't merit consideration.

But serious astrology has existed for thousands of years. H. J. Eysenck and D.K.B. Nias define it in their book *Astrology: Science or Superstition?*:

> This (traditional astrology) deals with the connections believed to exist between the positions of the planets at the moment of someone's birth and that person's character, development, profession, marriage and general life history. This type of astrology can be descriptive (trying to help someone understand himself) or predictive (trying to forecast what will happen to him) or postdictive (trying to interpret and make sense of his past life). Predictive astrology can also concern itself with broader issues, such as the fate of nations, treaties and battles, arguing from the position of the planets at the time the treaties were signed, the battles were joined, kings or presidents inaugurated, and so forth.[22]

After studying the subject thoroughly, the authors concluded that, while astrology might provide meaningful insight into an individual's existence, the discipline as a whole has problems. "The major failure to which we have returned time after time is the lack of replication. It is not enough for a second researcher to set off on a similar trail of his own. If he is to validate the original research he must replicate it *in the same form* ... A hypothesis must survive repeated attempts to break it down. Only then can we place reliance on it."[23] We're back to the problem we've encountered in trying to test ESP—lack of repeatability.

A second problem is that "there is not one astrology but several—European, Indian, Chinese—and different astrologers would therefore make different predictions from the same facts. In contrast, the laws of physics and astronomy are the same all over the world, and one would expect the same to be true of astrology if it did indeed have any factual basis. Science is international in its theories and findings, and astrology's failure to arrive at a set of universally agreed rules must speak heavily against it."[24]

Another problem is that people can interpret horoscopes to mean almost anything they want them to mean. One study of 38 college students demonstrates this. Each student was given two detailed horoscopes. One corresponded to his sign, the other was a "placebo"—a randomly selected horoscope from another sign. Of the 38 students, 22 rated their own horoscopes as accurate, 14 as inaccurate, and two said it was about even. As far as the placebo horoscopes, 19 rated them as accurate and 19, not accurate. In comparing the two horoscopes, 19 rated their own as more accurate than the placebo, 18 rated the placebo more accurate than their own, and one said they were even.[25]

Evidently people feel a need to know something about their future. I believe that God understands that need. That is why it is important to understand one more principle: *We need to evaluate all prophecies in light of Scripture.* The Bible clearly warns us about following after false prophets, sorcerers, diviners, mediums, etc. In Isaiah, God warned, "Let now the astrologers, those who prophesy by the stars, those who predict by the new moons, stand up and save you from what will come upon you. Behold, they have become like stubble, fire burns them; they cannot deliver themselves from the power of the flame."[26]

Jeremiah gave a similar warning: "Do not learn the way of the nations, and do not be terrified by the signs of the heavens although the nations are terrified by them; for the customs of the peoples are delusion."[27]

God laid down strict regulations concerning prophets. First, genuine prophets were to point people to the one true God. Joseph Smith failed here, in that he declared there were many gods.[28] Second, a genuine prophet cannot utter one false prophecy. Prophets of the Bible told short-term and long-term prophecies. The fulfillment of their short-term predictions validated their long-range prophecies. Third, the purpose of prophecy is to cause people to obey God's commands and to believe in His Son Jesus Christ.

The Bible contains numerous prophecies. Already many

have been literally fulfilled. More than three hundred of them concern the Messiah, and Jesus Christ fulfilled them. Other prophecies concern the end times, and we will look more at these in chapter 10. But it is important to realize why God gave us these words. They are not intended to satisfy our curiosity, but rather to help prepare us for the future, and to encourage and comfort us.[29]

Chapter Seven

NOT SO MYSTERIOUS MYSTERIES

Everyone likes a good mystery—just look at the sales of books by Von Daniken and Berlitz. There is always a substantial market for tabloids and paperback books with stories concerning the Bermuda Triangle, Unidentified Flying Objects, the lost civilization of Atlantis, and other mysterious phenomena.

In the mid-seventies, I started getting a number of questions about the Bermuda Triangle. Several movies and television shows had helped popularize it. I had discovered that attendance at my shows jumped dramatically when I dealt with popular mysteries, so I decided to research the subject. Unfortunately it would be difficult to gain firsthand experience on this subject as I had with other phenomena. I couldn't go out into the middle of the triangle and wait for something to happen, so I had to look for other sources.

In his best-seller, *The Bermuda Triangle*, Charles Berlitz defines the area in question:

> There is a section of the Western Atlantic, off the southeast coast of the United States, forming what has been termed a triangle, extending from Bermuda in the north to southern Florida, and then east to a point through the Bahamas past Puerto Rico to about 40 west longitude and then back again to Bermuda. This area occupies a disturbing and almost unbelievable place in the world's catalogue of unexplained mysteries. This is usually referred to as the Bermuda Triangle, where more than 100 planes and ships have literally vanished into thin air, most of them since 1945, and where more than 1,000 lives have been lost in the past twenty-six years, without a single body or even a piece of wreckage from the vanishing planes or ships having been found. Disappearances continue to occur with apparently increasing frequency, in spite of the fact that the seaways and airways are today more traveled, searches are more thorough, and records are more carefully kept.[1]

The author goes on to describe how planes have vanished while in radio contact with control towers, and how others had radioed "the most extraordinary messages, implying that they could not get their instruments to function, that their compasses were spinning, that the sky had turned yellow and hazy (on a clear day), and that the ocean . . .'didn't look right.' "[2] Boats, large and small, also have vanished without a trace. Others were found drifting, but with no survivors or bodies on board.

There have been numerous attempts to explain the mystery. Some of the explanations are extremely creative: sudden tidal waves, fireballs that explode the planes, a time-space warp, electromagnetic aberrations and attacks by UFOs.

I found the best source of information on this subject in my own neighborhood. His name is Larry Kusche, and when I met him he was on the faculty of Arizona State University, just a few miles from my home. His book, *The Bermuda Triangle Mystery—Solved,* was a masterpiece of investigative reporting. From Kusche I learned enough information to draw several conclusions.

First, *15 to 20 percent of the incidents reported about the Bermuda Triangle never even happened.*

Berlitz reported that in October of 1978, three people on a 40-foot cabin cruiser disappeared in clear weather and calm seas during a short trip between Bimini and Miami. Author Michael Dennett did a detailed investigation of this and other recent Triangle incidents:

> This case is, as Berlitz might describe it, a classic Bermuda Triangle disappearance. It has all the hallmarks of such an occurrence; namely, an unidentified vessel, with three unnamed people on board, vanishes on an unspecified date. The local newspaper carried no report of this incident and the Coast Guard was unable to confirm that a vessel matching this description had been lost in October.[3]

Second, *25 to 30 percent of the mysterious disappearances did not even take place within the boundaries of the Bermuda Triangle.*

When it suited their purposes, mystery writers included air and sea disasters in the Gulf of Mexico and the far reaches of the Atlantic ocean hundreds of miles outside the triangle borders. An American Globemaster that "disappeared north of the triangle in March 1950" actually exploded about 600 miles southwest of Ireland, at least 1,000 miles outside the Triangle.

Third, *those who describe most of the cases try to convince readers that the disappearances took place on calm, clear days, when in reality they took place in very severe weather.*

In the epilogue to his book *The Bermuda Triangle Mystery— Solved,* Kusche wrote:

> After examining all the evidence I have reached the following conclusion: *There is no theory that solves the mystery.* It is no more logical to try to find a common cause for all the disappearances in the Triangle than, for example, to try to find one cause for all automobile accidents in Arizona. By abandoning the search for an overall theory and investigating each incident independently, the mystery began to unravel.
>
> The findings of my research were consistent . . . .Once sufficient information was found, logical explanations appeared for most of the incidents. It is difficult, for example, to consider the *Rubicon* a mystery when it is known that a hurricane struck the harbor where it had been moored. It is similarly difficult to be baffled by the loss of the *Marine Sulphur Queen* after learning of the ship's weakened structure and the weather conditions as described in the report of the Coast Guard investigation.[4]

My final conclusion was that *the number of disappearances within the boundaries of the Bermuda Triangle are actually no greater than the number of disappearances in almost any other comparable part of the world.*

In an exclusive interview in the *Globe,* a national tabloid, Berlitz claimed that fifty planes and more than a hundred ships had vanished in two years, and that the government was conspiring to keep this information secret. Dennet found that only a dozen "unexplained" incidents occurred during a twenty-five-month period ending in January of 1980. He systematically reviewed all twelve of the incidents mentioned by Berlitz and found that, with sufficient information, most of the "mysteries" were solved.

It's surprising that Berlitz hasn't tackled another mystery. On an average of nearly once a month, a small, private airplane takes off from a United States airport and disappears. Despite searches, no debris is found. Everyone assumes that the lost plane crashed, but no one can find it. Occasionally it is found years later in some rugged mountains.

Bermuda Triangle writers make a big fuss over the fact that no debris is found. In fact, when flights are lost over water, debris rarely is found, especially if the crash is at night in rough seas. By the time morning light allows a search to begin, the seas have hidden all traces of a crash.

The popularity of the Bermuda Triangle mystery has spawned similar mysteries, such as the Devil's Sea near Japan and the Great Lakes Triangle. In my opinion, these mysteries exist only in the minds of those who make up and write the stories concerning them. These are further evidence that when anything, no matter how ridiculous, is presented in a serious manner, in an atmosphere where honesty is taken for granted, it can mislead even the most intelligent people if they do not investigate the facts.

To illustrate my point, I created an illusion for my show which I call "The Bermuda Triangle." After I seat myself inside a triangular box of lights, it is then closed. When the box is reopened, I have vanished. Most observers can't explain that illusion, but that doesn't make it any more authentic than these fabricated mysteries.

André's "Bermuda Triangle" illustration.

Probably the most famous mystery of the Bermuda Triangle was the disappearance of Flight 19. The legend makes for eerie reading. On December 5, 1945, five Avenger torpedo bombers took off from Fort Lauderdale Naval Air Station on a routine patrol. An hour and a half later, when they should have been starting their return to base, the flight commander reported he was lost over the Florida Keys, many miles from where he should have been. For the next few hours, frantic efforts were made to find the planes and guide them back home, but they never were located. In addition, a giant Mariner PBM search plane, called a flying boat, took off to try to find the Avengers and never returned. A five-day massive air and sea search turned up no evidence of the six planes.

Over the years the story became a legend, to the point where it was almost impossible to separate fact from fiction. Larry Kusche meticulously studied all the available information, including the official Naval investigations, and interviewed most of the surviving people involved in the incident to reconstruct what actually happened. His book *The Disappearance of Flight 19* is exciting reading, but it is hardly the "Twilight Zone" type of mystery that Berlitz and others would have us believe.

Kusche concluded that the five Avengers almost certainly were over the Bahamas—their intended target—and not the Florida Keys. An accomplished pilot himself, Kusche flew the intended route of Flight 19 and observed several reasons why a pilot could become disoriented. He noticed that a haze, caused by the humid air, can cause the sky and ocean to blend so that there appears to be no horizon. On that fateful day in 1945, visibility was less than ten miles and a slight error in navigation could cause the pilots to miss expected landmarks. Parts of the Bahamas and the Keys look remarkably alike. Thinking he was over the Keys, the leader, Chuck Taylor, apparently headed north in order to find the Florida mainland. But he never reached land. In the dark, with extremely rough seas, the planes ditched in the ocean approximately two hundred miles east of the Florida coast.

The disappearance of the search plane also can be explained logically:

> The loss of the Mariner PBM search plane came to be considered mysterious after storytellers had it "vanish" at

4:25 in a clear, sunlit sky, as it was "approaching the zone where Flight 19 had strangely disappeared." The 7:50 explosion, the story went, was yet another mystery.

Mariners were sometimes called "flying gas tanks" because they carried almost 2,000 gallons of fuel. Fumes were occasionally present inside the plane. The lighting of a cigarette, the flipping on of the PBM's unshielded electrical switches, the starting of the small auxiliary generator . . . any number of other activities could have provided the ignition. One officer I discussed this with told me that he had seen a Mariner explode while flying over an air base in Greece . . . .

Besides time warps and related so-called paranormal phenomena, other highly dramatic "theories" have been suggested to account for the Mariner's loss. One is that one or more of the Avengers had a midair collision with it. Another is that when Taylor gave one of his students permission to drop his last bomb, it hit the Mariner. Both guesses not only are extremely improbable, but also they do not correlate with what is known about the events of that day.[5]

Another mystery that has intrigued millions is that of unidentified flying objects (UFOs). A former president of the International Brotherhood of Magicians, Bill Pitts, is one of the leading investigators of UFOs. He has told me that there really are no authorities on the subject: "There are only authorities on reported sightings of UFOs. There are no authorities because we have not had, to my knowledge, one UFO that we could take pictures of and examine every nut and bolt on it, and interview the beings on the craft.

"I have been an investigator for many of the serious research organizations as well as for several government agencies. I periodically receive calls from law enforcement personnel and from radar control tower operators who are trying to explain unusual things." Pitts takes each case and tries to provide an explanation—to turn a UFO into an IFO, an identified flying object. "We can't do that in every case, but I try to find out what it could have been. I don't say this is definitely what they saw, because once it's gone, I don't know. But I have ways of finding out what it could have been. I carry with me phone numbers from FAA, control towers, various police departments,

Norad, etc."

The United States Air Force has conducted two exhaustive investigations and concluded that "there is no evidence for the existence of UFOs with supernatural, extraterrestrial, or military origin."[6] More than 90 percent of all UFO sightings can be attributed to purely natural causes.

Yet UFOs have become increasingly popular with movies such as *Close Encounters of the Third Kind* and *ET, the Extraterrestrial*. The number of UFO sightings increases markedly when movies like these are shown, or when the media report about a person who had a spectacular "encounter." The sensational publicity garnered from cases such as the alleged abduction of Travis Walton in November of 1975 in Arizona, result in further interest, and further distortion of the truth.

Jeff Wells, a reporter for the *National Enquirer*, was sent to Phoenix to interview Walton shortly after he claimed to have spent five days aboard an alien spacecraft. Wells reported that the most experienced polygraph examiner in Arizona gave Walton a lie detector test, but the results were not revealed in the *National Enquirer*. "The kid had failed the test miserably," wrote Wells later. "The polygraph man said it was the plainest case of lying he'd seen in 20 years."

Much of Walton's story developed during hypnosis sessions. "It seemed that the kid's father, who had deserted him as a child, had been a spaceship fanatic, and all his life the kid had wanted to ride in a spacecraft. He had seen something out there in the woods, some kind of an eerie light that had triggered a powerful hallucination....There was no question of any kidnap by mushroom men. The kid needed medical help."[0]

Philip J. Kass has done extensive research in this area. In his book, *UFOs Explained*, he gives some very sensible explanations for the UFO phenomenon. The following is a sample of his "UFOlogical principles":

> Basically honest and intelligent persons who are suddenly exposed to a brief, unexpected event, especially one that involves an unfamiliar object, may be grossly inaccurate in trying to describe precisely what they have seen.

> The problem facing the UFO investigator is to try to distinguish between those details that are accurate and

Chapter Eight

LOOK INTO MY EYES

To the sound of music, my daughter Robyn walks on stage. Dramatically waving my fingers over her eyes, I appear to put her into a trance. Then she is assisted as she climbs into a box, and I proceed to saw her in half.

In another part of my show, I seem to put myself into a trance as I sit in front of a circle of lights. Concentrating intently, I slowly begin to rise into the air. The levitation appears to result from my hypnotic state.

I'm going to let you in on a secret. When you see me hypnotized or hypnotizing someone else on stage, it's all for show. No one is actually in a trance. I dare say that is true for most stage magicians. It's simply good showmanship—something expected of illusionists.

An aura of mystery surrounds hypnotism. Many books have been written on the subject, yet most people still misunderstand it. Many think it can do more than it actually can, while others think it is a tool of the devil. It has been used effectively in place of drugs for anesthesia in dentistry and minor surgery, and as a tool to help people break habits such as smoking.

The father of modern hypnotism was Anton Mesmer, an eighteenth century German physician. Through controversial experiments, he tried to prove the existence of magnetic fluids in his patients. Using magnets, he attempted to cure physical illnesses. Later he set aside the magnets and used methods such as waving his hands over a patient until the patient went into a trance. Surprisingly, many of his patients found relief from their symptoms through his unorthodox practices. The term "animal magnetism" and the field of study called "mesmerism" resulted from his work.

In the 1800s, British surgeon James Braid coined the term "hypnotism" when he induced his patients into a sleeplike condition before performing minor operations. The word comes from the Greek word "hypnos" meaning sleep. Later Dr. Braid realized that he had misnamed the phenomenon, for a hypnotized person definitely is not sleeping. But it was too late to change it, as the general public readily.

The simplest way to understand hypnosis is to regard it as a state of mind characterized by increased suggestibility—the acceptance of an idea without being critical of the idea. It is a method for bypassing the conscious mind. Unlike the conscious, the subconscious mind has no power to discriminate. The subconscious is the memory's storehouse, recording every experience from earliest infancy. Whatever is presented to it under certain conditions, such as hypnotism, automatically is accepted and acted upon.

Psychologist Ray Hyman says that when it comes to clearly defining hypnotism, no one really knows what it is. "The only way we have of knowing someone was hypnotized is if that person says he was. There is no external way of measuring the hypnotic state—there is no physiological sign on which everyone can agree."

Hypnotism is used in a number of ways. Some entertainers hypnotize members of the audience and cause them to do

While André was in India he visited a snake charmer. Contrary to what most people think the snake does not rise because it is hypnotized by the music of the flute. The snake cannot even hear the music. The truth is that the fakir simply teases the snake by tapping the basket, and the vibrations make the snake rise.

84

unusual, humorous things that they normally would not do. Another widespread use of hypnotism is for medical purposes—to block pain and to help patients break bad habit patterns. Hypnotism also is used for interrogation, although we'll see later that there are serious questions about its effectiveness. We've all seen or heard stories about hypnotists wielding tremendous powers over their subjects. Some movies and novels have portrayed hypnotists dominating weaker minds and using their power for evil purposes. This may be true in movies or books, but in this case real life does not match fiction.

To understand what hypnotism is, it helps to know what it *cannot* do. For instance, *you cannot be hypnotized against your will.* To be hypnotized, the patient must want to be hypnotized and must trust the hypnotist. Peter Blythe wrote in his book on hypnotism:

> If someone says, "Go ahead and see if you can hypnotize me," the answer is that you cannot. The person who makes the statement is challenging the hypnotist; and as he intends to resist, any chance of success is aborted from the outset.
>
> When one gentleman first started using hypnosis he tried out various induction methods on his wife, but without any result. She knew they worked on other people, because she had seen them being applied, but she resisted because she felt no need to cooperate.
>
> Then on a hot summer's day she fell asleep in the garden while sunbathing, and as a result was quite badly sunburned.
>
> That same night she tried to sleep, but her skin was so tender that sleep eluded her.
>
> After tossing and turning for more than an hour she asked her husband, "Could you hypnotize me, and take the pain away so that I can get some sleep?"
>
> At that moment she discovered a need for hypnosis and quickly allowed her critical censor to be by-passed, and entered into the hypnotic state.[1]

Another misconception is that a person under hypnosis can be forced to do things that violate his moral values.

A person under hypnosis remains conscious of what the hypnotist says and does. He usually willingly submits to the hypnotist, doing what he instructs and accepting his sugges-

85

tions. But *if the hypnotist inserts a command or suggestion against the patient's will, the patient will not respond.*

Blythe gives an interesting example of this:

> Four people were on the stage in the hypnotic state and were carrying out the various suggestions of the hypnotist. Then, at a certain point, he suggested they were all concert pianists and were going to give a piano recital. Three of the subjects actetd out this suggestion, one with greater aplomb than the other two; but the only lady on the stage just sat on her chair, deeply relaxed, and did nothing ....
>
> I talked to the lady after the demonstration and asked her why she had chosen not to react to that piano-playing suggestion. Her answer was personal, but very logical. She told me that as a small child she had been made to take piano lessons against her will, but as soon as she was old enough to exert some pressure on her parents she stopped playing, and made a promise to herself that nothing would ever induce her to play again.[2]

Third, *information gained through hypnosis may not be any more accurate than other forms of interrogation.*

This area is controversial. Some states allow evidence gained through hypnosis to be used in court. Others do not. Dr. Martin Orne, editor of the *International Journal of Clinical and Experimental Hypnosis,* explains the problem: "You don't ever know whether you have testimony created by hypnosis or whether it was in fact refreshed by hypnosis. Until we have hard evidence of the differences between these two things, we can't distinguish between helping an eyewitness to remember what he saw versus creating an eyewitness who never was."[3]

The problem is evident particularly in UFO cases where evidence gained under hypnosis is displayed as conclusive proof. Orne states that under hypnotism the most accurate information comes from "free narrative recall," but this produces the lowest amount of detail. When questioned about details, accuracy decreases. "Hypnotic suggestions to relive a past event, particularly when accompanied by questions about specific details, put pressure on the subject to provide information for which few, if any, actual memories are available. This situation may jog the subject's memory and produce some increased recall, but it will also cause him to fill in details that are plausible but consist of memories or fantasies from other times . . . .It is extremely difficult to know which aspects of hypnotically aided recall are historically accurate and which aspects have been confabulated."[4]

Further difficulties arise if the hypnotist has specific beliefs about what actually occurred. It is easy for him to inadvertently guide the subject's recall to fit his own beliefs. Ernest R. Hilgard, professor emeritus of psychology at Stanford University and former president of the International Society of Hypnosis, claims that hypnotic recall, as evidence of UFO abduction, is an abuse of hypnosis. He explains how it is possible to fabricate stories:

> For example, under hypnosis I implanted in a subject a false memory of an experience connected with a bank robbery that never occurred, and the person found the experience so vivid that he was able to select from a series of photographs a picture of the man he thought had robbed the bank.
>
> At another time, I deliberately assigned two concurrent—though spatially very different—life experiences to the same person and regressed him at separate times to that date. He gave very accurate accounts of both experiences, so that a believer in reincarnation, reviewing the two accounts, would have suspected that the man had really lived the two assigned lives.[5]

Hypnotism can be used for good or evil. The danger is that when you submit to hypnosis, you actually give control of yourself and your mind to another individual. So one should be extremely cautious about whom he submits himself to.

To be effective, hypnotism requires faith. One can get similar effects through certain vitamin pills, a charismatic healer, exercise, etc. Hypnotism is not some magic formula—it's effectiveness depends on the patient's faith.

I have seen this demonstrated in primitive cultures. For example, a witch doctor in Liberia put a curse on a person, and the victim took it so seriously that he went out of the village, lay down and died. That same witch doctor became furious with me and cursed me, but it had no effect whatsoever because I did not believe him or his powers. Missionaries there have told me they've had to talk people out of curses they believed were placed on them.

In a sense this validates some statements Ray Hyman made to me in an interview at his home. He said that the same results obtained through hypnotism can be gained without hypnotism. Dr. Hyman explains, "There have been studies done on this, and they've found that with the right motivation, a patient can do the same things without hypnosis that he can with it. For example, take the area of pain tolerance. They'll take one group of subjects, hypnotize them and stick needles in them, and they won't wince. The second group is offered a sum of money and told that someone will stick needles in them and they are to act as if nothing is happening. Then they bring in trained hypnotists and they can't tell the difference."

Undoubtedly there is a hypnotic state, but experts have difficulty defining it. They can measure brain waves and tell when a person is asleep. They also can determine when a person is dreaming. But there is no comparable measurement of the hypnotic state.

"Some people will play the role," Hyman says. "In given circumstances, they will try to figure out 'what's expected of

In 1978 André took part in a televised debate in Nigeria with two men from a spiritualistic church—they talked about communicating with the dead.

me' and behave that way. They will even do things they would never do under normal circumstances. Some psychologists argue that this is because they really wanted to do those things, and this just gave them an excuse. Most hypnotists will tell you that a person will not do something under hypnosis that he really doesn't want to do. He will resist or come out of the hypnotic state."

Technically hypnosis is not in the realm of the paranormal, but people claim to use it in that realm. They allegedly contact the dead, read minds, predict the future and do other feats while in a hypnotic trance. In fact, though, the trance usually is a cover-up to justify their activities.

In the field of hypnosis, as in the other areas we have explored, many questions remain unanswered. We could spend hundreds more pages examining the world of illusion in greater detail, but would we come any closer to the truth?

For many years William James was a leading researcher of psychic phenomena. Shortly before his death, he said he was still just as confused about the subject as when he started. He suggested that maybe the good Lord meant it that way. Maybe He wanted to leave enough tantalizing evidence to show that there might be something there, but He didn't want us to know for sure.

Despite the confusion in this area, people still look for answers from mediums, fortune tellers, faith healers and astrologers. They search for something to give them hope and direction, and they will find it in the realm of psychic phenomena, but it is only an illusion. For true answers, they must return to the world of reality.

That is where we will now turn our attention. In the next few chapters we will focus on truth, rather than illusions. We will examine what I consider to be the ultimate reality.

Chapter Nine

MAGICIAN OR GOD?

We have examined the feats and claims of a number of people. We briefly explored the world of spiritism, the "miracles" of psychic healers, the magic of mind reading, the not-so-amazing modern-day prophets, and other incredible feats and stories that don't stand the test of close scrutiny. As a magician, I conclude that any "supernatural" phenomenon I have witnessed can be explained—by thoroughly checking all the facts—as either trickery or deception, or as a normal predictable psychological response.

Then what about the person of Jesus Christ? I shared in chapter 2 how Christ became a reality in my life. How does He differ from all the charlatans and tricksters we have examined? Was He truly a miracle worker, or was He only a clever magician? Jesus Christ claimed to be God. Does His life match His claim?

These questions confronted me as a young man and I faced two possibilities. If Jesus Christ was *not* God—He claimed that He was—and if what He said was not true, then Christianity makes little difference. But if He was and is God, and if what He says is true, then very little else makes any difference.

A clever magician easily can fool a scientist, professor, theologian or anyone else. Most people do not think like magicians, and they do not understand all of the psychology and methods we use to fool our audiences. It is very difficult, however, for one experienced magician to fool another experienced magician. Because of my extensive knowledge concerning the art of magic, I concluded that I might be the most qualified to determine if the miraculous events attributed to Christ could have been accomplished by trickery, or if they were indeed genuine.

I will not attempt to ascertain if the gospel events were accurately reported. Numerous studies already conclusively

91

demonstrate the reliability of biblical documents.[1] So I will assume their validity and concentrate on the miracles of Christ. I analyzed these for several months before I became convinced of their authenticity.

The first thing that impressed me about the miracles of Jesus of Nazareth was their uniqueness. When we trace any subject's history from its origin, we usually find slow, gradual development over many centuries. Then it begins to accelerate at an ever-increasing rate. We start with the simple and move to the complex.

That certainly is true of magic. Magic done through misdirection and sleight of hand is one of the oldest forms of entertainment known to man. Various forms of magic also were associated with worship in many pagan temples. But it wasn't until the seventeenth century, primarily through the creativity of Robert-Houdin, that large-scale stage illusions were developed. In the 20th century we have seen an explosion of knowledge, as magicians constantly have refined and developed the magical arts.

If Jesus Christ was a magician, then His illusions were totally different from anything any other magicians have done before or since, as you will see as we examine five of His miracles.

Jesus' first recorded miracle was at the wedding in Cana of Galilee, when the host ran out of wine.[2] In the Gospel of John we read that six stone waterpots were set aside for the Jewish custom of purification. Jesus commanded that these 20- to 30-gallon pots be filled with water. After the pots were filled, Jesus commanded the servants to draw out some of the water and take it to the headwaiter. When he tasted the "water which had become wine," he told the bridegroom that normally hosts served the best wine first, but the bridegroom had saved the best until then.

Jesus might have fooled a few people with a simple trick, perhaps using a chemical to change the color and taste of the water, but there was no way He could have done that with 120 to 180 gallons of water. He could not have fooled all of those guests into thinking that it was some of the finest wine they'd ever tasted.

On several occasions, I have been asked to perform before

magicians' conventions. One time a convention host asked me to perform on the beach before 700 magicians from around the world. He wanted me to create an illusion in which I would get out of a boat and walk on the water a short distance to land. After spending many weeks trying to formulate all the methods we could use for such an illusion, it finally was scrapped. It was impossible to create any type of effect that would convince anyone I really was walking on water.

This experience showed me that, even with all of our modern technology, we can't come close to duplicating many of the things Jesus did nearly 20 centuries ago. In Mark 6, we read about Jesus walking to the disciples on the Sea of Galilee, where they were straining at the oars because of the wind. The Sea of Galilee gets very rough under such conditions, yet in the midst of the waves, Jesus walked to the boat. When film-makers have used trick photography to portray this event in movies about Christ, the results have been pathetic.

One miracle recorded in all four gospels is the feeding of the 5,000. The writers all record the presence of 5,000 men, not counting women and children. It is reasonable to suppose that Christ actually fed 15,000 to 20,000 people with five loaves of bread and two small fish.

A few years ago I produced a show presenting some of the greatest events in the life of Christ. Now I am working on a new version of the show, which will include a staged recreation of this miracle. The audience will see the bread visibly multiply in the hands of "Jesus," and then actors playing the disciples will pass out the bread. Every person in the auditorium will receive a good sized piece of the bread either to eat or to take home as a reminder of that experience.

But you can do many things on a stage that you cannot do out in the open. Jesus was outdoors, with no stage protecting Him. He certainly could not have hid that much food up his sleeves! To do such a trick and fool so many people about the source of the bread would have required the disciples' involvement in the deception. And if indeed the disciples participated in that trick, then why do we never hear any more about it? None of them ever even hinted at collaboration to produce such a marvelous miracle.

All except one of the original apostles died a martyr's death for witnessing to the deity of Christ. Throughout history, people have willingly died for a lie when they did not know it was a lie. But it is contrary to all human experience for a group of men to die as martyrs, claiming that a lie was the truth when they knew differently. I do not believe Jesus' feeding of the 5,000 was a trick.

If Jesus simply had been a magician, performing the miracles He did would have required two or three semi trucks full of equipment, plus numerous assistants. When I do a major show, I require 20 to 30 assistants backstage and two truckloads of equipment. Yet Jesus had none of that.

The two other miracles I will mention involve healing. Was Jesus any different from modern-day psychic and faith healers, who cure mostly psychosomatic illnesses?

It is recorded that Jesus healed men who were blind from birth, people who were born deaf and dumb, lepers in advanced stages of decay, a woman who had had a hemorrhage for a dozen years, and a man who was lame from birth. These types of physical problems cannot be classified as psychosomatic illness.

The writer of the Gospel of Luke was a physician and he carefully recorded many of the miraculous healings. In Luke 6 we read about a man in the synagogue whose right hand was withered. While the scribes and Pharisees watched him closely, Jesus told the man to hold out his hand and it "was completely restored." How could that have been a feat of magic? Everyone knew the man. Christ's enemies were watching every move. I have never seen or heard of any documented case where a psychic healer performed such a miracle.

One more miracle bears mentioning: Jesus raised men from the dead. One such incident occurs in John 11. Lazarus, a close friend of Jesus, died and was buried in the typical Jewish manner of the day. After washing the body with soap and water, they made a final test to assure he was not breathing. Then they wrapped the body in long strips of linen cloth, about six feet in length. They started at the feet, wrapping the legs, and between the wraps they put a very sticky syrup-like substance made of myrrh and aloes. This preserved the body. They wrapped each leg and arm separately, and then the trunk. Gradually the gummy paste, mixed in with the cloth, hardened. A man of Lazarus's stature in the community might have been encased in more than a hundred pounds of material and spices.

After the body was prepared it was laid in a cave, which then was sealed with a large rock so animals would not disturb it. No one doubted that the person was dead by the time he was laid in a cave.

Jesus arrived on the scene four days after Lazarus had died. Family and friends were still mourning. When Jesus asked them to roll the stone from the cave, Martha, one of Lazarus's sisters, protested that the body would stink from the decay. Nevertheless they removed the stone. Then Jesus, with a loud voice, called, "Lazarus, come forth."

Then we read, "He who had died came forth, bound hand and foot with wrappings; and his face was wrapped around with a cloth. Jesus said to them, 'Unbind him, and let him go.' "[3] Many of the Jews who were with the sisters when Lazarus died believed in Jesus as a result of what He did.

We could examine many other examples of Jesus' miracles. Anyone honestly investigating His works would have to conclude from all the evidence that Jesus had supernatural ability.

Another factor that played a major role in my conclusions concerning Jesus Christ was His fulfillment of the more than 300 Old Testament references to the Messiah. These include: He would be born in Bethlehem, He would be in the direct line of King David, a special prophet would immediately precede His arrival (John the Baptist), He would heal the blind and deaf, He would be betrayed for 30 pieces of silver, His death would be by crucifixion among thieves, His executioners would cast lots for His clothing, He would be buried in a rich man's tomb, and He would rise from the dead three days after His burial.

I was impressed by how detailed these prophecies were. One person conceivably might fulfill two or three of these, but not this many. Peter Stoner in his book *Science Speaks* shows statistically that it was virtually beyond the realm of chance that one man would fulfill even eight of the prophecies:

> . . . We find that the chance that any man might have lived down to the present time and fulfilled all eight prophecies is 1 in 10^{17} . . . This is illustrated by taking 10^{17} silver dollars and laying them on the face of Texas. They

will cover all of the state two feet deep. Now mark one of these silver dollars and stir the whole mass thoroughly, all over the state. Blindfold a man and tell him he can travel as far as he wishes, but he must pick up one silver dollar and say that this is the right one. What chance could he have of getting the right one? Just the same chance that the prophets would have had of writing these eight prophecies and having all come true in any one man . . . provided they wrote them in their own wisdom. Now these prophecies were either given by inspiration of God or the prophets just wrote them as they thought they should be. In such a case the prophets had just one chance in 10^{17} of being absolute.[4]

The Bible prophecies concerning end times were another major factor in my conversion, because if they were accurate, they lent credibility to the rest of the Scripture. I spent many hours on this area of investigation.

Numerous prophecies in the Bible concern the return of Christ to this earth. The disciples specifically asked Him, "Tell us . . . what will be the sign of Your coming, and of the end of the age?"[5] The Bible contains so many references to the second coming of Christ that it can be said that the major part of Scripture deals with this event. It is mentioned 380 times in the New Testament alone.

Before leaving the earth, Jesus told His disciples that He would physically return to earth at a future time in history when mankind was on the verge of destroying the entire human race. When His followers asked Him when this would be, He said it was not for them to know the day or the hour, but He would give them a number of signs.

I found 27 specific signs relating to the end times and the physical return of Jesus Christ to the earth. They include such things as the regathering of the people of Israel in the Middle East, the rise of Russia and China, the European Common Market, an explosion of knowledge, extensive traveling, increased lawlessness and many more.

To me, the most significant sign was the rebirth of the nation of Israel. When I first read about that, I was shocked because for 2,600 years there was no nation of Israel. Yet Ezekiel, Daniel, Hosea, Zechariah and Jeremiah all wrote that the final war would begin in and be centered around that nation. Jesus said that the city of Jerusalem "will be trampled underfoot by the Gentiles until the times of the Gentiles be fulfilled."[6] Jerusalem was controlled by Gentiles from 586 B.C. until June, 1967. Then, in a six-day war, the Jews, outnumbered eighty to one, captured the city of Jerusalem, bringing the times of the Gentiles to an end.

Looking at even just a few other prophecies gives us an idea of the incredible accuracy of the Bible. Jesus said, "You will be hearing of wars and rumors of wars. . . For nation will rise against nation, and kingdom against kingdom, and in various places there will be famines and earthquakes."[7]

Of course, there always have been wars, famines and earthquakes. But Jesus said that just before the end they suddenly would increase in intensity and frequency. He compared this to the intensity and frequency of contractions just before a woman gives birth to a child. In World War I, about 8,500,000 were killed. In World War II, an estimated 52,000,000 were killed. In 1945 the United Nations was founded for the purpose of helping preserve peace throughout the world. Since then there have been 150 wars and more than 10,000,000 people killed. As I write today, there are 14 wars going on in some part of the world. Dag Hammarskjold, former Secretary General of the United Nations, said shortly before his death that he saw no hope for a permanent world peace without a spiritual rebirth. With the nuclear age, man now has the capacity through one bomb to exceed the entire destructive power of all the bombs dropped during World War II. As part of His end times prophecy, Christ said, "Unless those days had been cut short, no life would have been saved, but for the sake of the elect those days shall be cut short."[8]

It is also interesting that Peter describes the return of Christ like this: "The heavens will pass away with a roar and the elements will be destroyed with intense heat, and the earth and its works will be burned up."[9] Until the atom bomb came along, scientists scoffed at these and other similar verses. The Bible, written 2,000-3,000 years ago, is more relevant and up to date than tomorrow's newspaper.

Regarding famine, two-thirds of the world does not have enough to eat. Hal Lindsey, author of *The Late Great Planet*

Earth, reports, "Many experts say the age of the famines began in 1974. In that year, terrible shortages broke out in parts of Africa and Asia. Even when emergency food supplies were sent, the starving millions didn't receive them in time."[10]

Christ also mentioned an increase in earthquakes. From 1900 to 1969, there were 28 major earthquakes, each claiming more than 100 lives. From 1970-79, there were 20 major quakes.[11] Hal Lindsey adds, "The 1970s experienced the largest increase in the number of killer quakes known to history. In fact, the dramatic increase in quakes in 1976 led many scientists to say we are entering a period of great seismic disturbances."[12]

If Christ's miracles, His fulfillment of Old Testament prophecy, and His accurate foretelling of 20th century life were not enough, His own resurrection—which He predicted several times—finally proved to me His deity. In His death He suffered the ultimate in physical cruelty and torture. First the Romans stripped Him, tied him down, then beat his back with a whip that had pieces of bone and metal tied in its leather thongs. The scourging literally tore the skin off His back and left Him near death.

Then He was crucified—the most hideous form of execution ever devised. Its purpose was not just to kill a person, but to prolong the suffering as long as possible. It often took three days for a person to die. Frederic W. Farrar described the suffering: "A death by crucifixion seems to include all that pain and death can have of horrible and ghastly—dizziness, cramp, thirst, starvation, sleeplessness, traumatic fever, tetanus, shame, publicity of shame, long continuance of torment, horror of anticipation, mortification of untended wounds—all intensified just up to the point at which they can be endured at all, but all stopping just short of the point which would give to the sufferer the relief of unconsciousness."[13]

Jesus was buried in the same manner as Lazarus was, and then a Roman guard was placed around the tomb at the insistence of the Jewish leaders who feared the disciples might steal the body.

Three days later the tomb was empty, and the entire course of history was altered. Numerous theories have been proposed to explain away His resurrection—the disciples went to the wrong tomb, Jesus didn't really die, the body was stolen—but none of them stand up under scrutiny.

After carefully examining the evidence of the resurrection, many have determined that it is one of the best documented events of history. In his book *More than a Carpenter,* Josh McDowell writes: "A student at the University of Uruguay said to me, 'Professor McDowell, why can't you refute Christianity?' I answered, 'For a very simple reason. I'm unable to explain away an event in history—the resurrection of Jesus Christ.'

"After more than 700 hours of studying this subject and thoroughly investigating its foundation, I came to the conclusion that the resurrection of Jesus Christ is either one of the most wicked, vicious, heartless hoaxes ever foisted upon people, or it is the most important fact of history."[14]

Josh gives voluminous support to verify Christ's resurrection as a historical fact. Here is just one example: "While professor of law at Harvard, [Dr. Simon] Greenleaf wrote a volume in which he examined the legal value of the apostles' testimony to the resurrection of Christ. He observed that it was impossible that the apostles could have persisted in affirming the truths they had narrated, had not Jesus actually risen from the dead, and had they not known this fact as certainly as they knew any other fact. Greenleaf concluded that the resurrection of Christ was one of the best supported events in history, according to the laws of legal evidence administered in courts of justice."[15]

The conclusion from my study was inescapable. I could not argue with His miracles. To re-enact them as an illusionist would cost several million dollars, and it would be very obvious that they were being accomplished through stage effects. I had to agree with Nicodemus, who said to Jesus, "We know that You have come from God . . . for no one can do these signs [miracles] that you do unless God is with him."[16]

Likewise I was convinced that His prophecies were not like those of Nostradamus, who told riddles that people could interpret only after the fact, some hitting and others missing. Jesus never missed. I can believe those prophecies that haven't been fulfilled yet because He's been right on every single one up until now. Only God has that kind of accuracy.

Through the centuries since His resurrection, men and women have studied this man to learn for themselves if He is indeed the Son of God. The exiled emperor Napoleon, on the lonely isle of St. Helena, said to his faithful General Bertrand, who did not believe in the deity of Jesus:

> I know men and I tell you that Jesus Christ is no mere man. Between Him and every other person in the world there is no possible term of comparison. Alexander, Caesar, Charlemagne, and I have founded empires. But on what did we rest the creations of our genius? Upon force. Jesus Christ founded His empire upon love; and at this hour millions of men would die for Him.[17]

But everyone must choose for himself. This is illustrated by a place in the Apline Mountains of Switzerland where you can stand, holding three blocks of wood. Throw one block in one direction and it floats down the little streams, into the Danube River and eventually into the Black Sea. Throw the second block of wood in a different direction and it finds its way to the Rhone River and eventually to the Mediterranean Sea. Throw the third block in another direction and it travels down the mountain streams into the Rhine River, which empties into the North Sea. *The decision of a moment can determine a destiny.*

A good friend of mine once said, "André, as you go through life, if you miss Christ, then you've missed it all." What we do with Jesus Christ is our most important decision. The rest of our lives—and our eternal destiny—depend upon that decision.

On March 13, 1982, André Kole received the highest award in his profession, a Performing Arts Fellowship, from the Academy of Magical Arts in Hollywood, California.

Chapter Ten

CALLED TO SERVE

The mail was piled several inches high on my desk when I returned from a long tour. I quickly sorted through it, setting aside a few business letters that required immediate attention. As I neared the bottom of the pile, one envelope caught my eye. It bore the insignia of the Magic Castle in Hollywood, one of the most successful night clubs in southern California. The old, mysterious looking building, located on a hill right above the former Grauman's Chinese Theater on Hollywood Boulevard, had become world famous for its creative and entertaining magical atmosphere.

The envelope contained a letter from the Magic Castle's president, William Larsen. Acting as a member of the board of directors for the Academy of Magical Arts, he informed me that I had been elected to receive a Performing Arts Fellowship—the highest award offered by my profession. It represents overall recognition for a lifetime of outstanding contributions to the field of magic. Larsen was inviting me to a gala dinner during which my award would be presented.

I leaned back in my chair, stunned by the news. Twenty years ago, when my goal was to become a world-renowned magician, this would have been a dream come true. Now the award brought satisfaction, but I felt no elation. That again proved to me that God truly had changed my motivations.

After becoming a Christian, I lost all desire to perform for fame or financial gain. I had seen enough of the show business world to know that some of the most disillusioned people were entertainers who had reached the top of their profession, expecting their success to bring them happiness. I had learned that was not reality.

I thought back to the decision I made in 1963—to devote my life and talents to serving God. For months I had struggled to know what to do with my unique skills. Several well-meaning

103

Christians advised me to give up magic and become a preacher. They said that God denounces all forms of magic. So I spent several weeks studying what the Bible says about various forms of magic. I learned that God specifically condemns:

Diviners: people who seek to obtain secret knowledge of past, present and especially future events, supposedly through communication with demons.

Soothsayers: those who predict the future by observing the flight or actions of birds and omens.

Enchanters: men who subdue others through charms or spells.

Witches (also translated sorcerers): people who use supernatural means or the aid of evil spirits to accomplish unusual feats, or who make a pact with the devil or evil spirits.

Mediums: people who claim to be able to communicate with the dead.

Wizards: those adept in the black art, or the art of accomplishing feats by supernatural means, often with the aid of evil spirits.

I realized that none of these described what I did. A magician is an artist who applies *natural* causes, whose operation is secret, to produce surprising effects. Everything I do as a magician is to entertain or instruct and is accomplished by natural means that usually involve much work and practice.

Still I struggled with how magic would fit into my life. One night, feeling completely miserable, I finally reached the point where I told God, "I will go anywhere You want me to go. I will do anything You want me to do." And I really meant those words, even if they meant I would never be involved in magic again. My heart felt strangely warm. I felt a wonderful peace— the same feeling I'd had many years before while walking to church in Santa Monica, California. That night, at the age of 25, I knew I had found the answer to my frustrating, empty existence.

That struggle taught me a most important lesson. *All of us have to come to the point where we're willing to give up what we're afraid God might want us to give up. Only then can He begin to really use us.* I realized that God doesn't look for great ability; He looks for usability. Soon afterward, the doors opened for me to use my talent to help bring others into a personal relationship with God. God seemed to tell me that He would rather I be a first-rate magician for Him than a second-rate preacher.

During this time I became involved in Campus Crusade for Christ, a non-demoninational Christian movement, at Arizona State University. I figured if any one group would resist spiritual matters, it was college students. Yet these were tomorrow's leaders, and therefore the most strategic group with which to share my discoveries.

Once while visiting my old fraternity, I heard a speaker get attention effectively through several excellent jokes. I wondered why I couldn't use magic for the same purpose. So I developed a program of magic and testimony to present to dormitories, fraternities, sororities and other campus groups. Several people responded to the invitation to know Christ personally, and I soon realized that students . were interested in spiritual truth. They were not interested in religion, but they were interested in Jesus Christ.

I began to see how I could use magic to present Christian truth, and I became captivated by a challenge far greater than that of entertaining. No business, adventure or profession could begin to match the challenge of the Great Commission, Jesus Christ's final instructions to His disciples: "All authority has been given to Me in heaven and on earth. Go therefore and make disciples of all the nations, baptizing them in the name of the Father and the Son and the Holy Spirit, teaching them to observe all that I commanded you; and lo, I am with you always, even to the end of the age."[1]

Bill Bright, president of Campus Crusade for Christ, has often said: "Only Christ offers a challenge worthy of total commitment. It is the one cause that demands the best that is in man, and which in turn accomplishes the most for the good of all men." That vision captivated me.

Many of our friends did not understand when my wife and I explained our decision to sell our businesses, leave the entertainment world and spend time with college students and laymen who were seeking reality in a confusing world. I could only say that it was similar to the Coast Guardsmen who prepared for a rescue attempt of two fishermen lost in a storm off the coast of Maine. As they were about to set out into the storm, they heard someone say over the howling winds and the roaring waves, "Don't go out there. You may never get back." One of the guardsmen replied, "We don't have to get back. But we have got to go." Almost two thousand years ago, Jesus Christ gave the Great Commission to *go* into all the world and to share the gospel with every person, so I had to go. But I didn't have to "get back," for this would be my life's work.

In the nearly twenty years since that decision, nothing had diminished the conviction with which I held my call. Serving as an ambassador for Christ had taken me to all fifty states and to seventy-six countries. I had performed on national television in forty countries and had audiences with monarchs and presidents, all for the purpose of presenting the person of Jesus Christ through magic.

I thought about the opportunities I'd had to return to show business. During my first year in ministry, a nightclub owner offered me a good deal of money—equal to two months salary in my new work—to perform at his club on New Year's Eve. I couldn't help but think of the millions of people who would celebrate New Year's Eve in thousands of nightclubs across the country, only to return the following day to their lives of nightmare and frustration—a new year, but the same old lives. So I spent that New Year's Eve at a party for college students, presenting the reality of new life in Jesus Christ.

I had other opportunities, but they, too, were easy to turn down. I only had to look at the letters and notes from men and women whose lives were being changed. Like the college student who wrote, "You saved my life. If I had not heard this message tonight, I would have committed suicide." Or the coed in Portland, Oregon, who wrote this letter:

> ... Last night my whole life changed. I heard Andre Kole speak in Portland and for the first time in my life I accepted Jesus Christ as my personal Savior. Never before had I experienced anything like this. My life has been more like dying than living. I have used and abused drugs ... was an honor student in high school ... at 19 was arrested on three felony counts, for sale and possession of narcotics. When I turned 21 last month, I felt more like being buried than coming of age. But something deep inside drew me to the ... meeting .... Last night when I

heard Andre speak, I truly believed for the first time and asked Christ to come into my life. This is a step I have tried to make for the last three years but failed to do alone.

I had so many memories. After a campus meeting in Sacramento, a Buddhist priest approached me and said, "I came today to see your magic, but after hearing your message I know I cannot continue with my present plans. My life will never be the same." A few months later, I heard that he had returned home to Japan to work with a Protestant church.

I thought of the university professor who talked to me after a program. For many years he had been looking for meaning and purpose for his own life. He said he had moved from Philadelphia to Washington state "to try to get away from it all and have some time to think." Then he said, "I believe God brought me three thousand miles just to hear this message tonight. This is what I have been looking for all of these years."

A midwestern doctor had written: "On October 30, 1971, I gave my heart to Christ on the campus of Northern Illinois University. An illusionist named André Kole presented a program touching the depths of my soul, a challenge to choose my eternal destiny. Jesus was and is the fulfillment of all my spiritual desires and thirsts. I want to thank you for introducing me to your best friend . . . .On my den wall I have my degree proudly framed. Next to it are the framed news clippings of André's visit—a kind of spiritual birth certificate!"

Another letter told me, "This December will be my tenth spiritual birthday . . . .When you told the story of the train coming down the mountain side as the drawbridge caretaker lowered the bridge, knowing it meant the death of his son . . . I felt as if I'd been slapped. Everything you said showed me that I'd been going through my life, simply waving merrily at God!"

I experienced numerous adventures in the course of seeing these results. Many unruly crowds were eager to heckle and disrupt my presentations, but every time, God's Spirit produced a "holy hush" when the time came to present Christ. Before I spoke at Harvard, one person said that my message was too simple for those intellectual students. That night 350 students crammed into a small dining room. Fifty-seven made decisions for Christ; another sixty asked for more information. I was told it made the greatest spiritual impact on that campus in twenty years.

Another time I spoke at Amherst College in Massachusetts. As I was about to walk on stage, a group of hooded Ku-Klux-Klan-type figures in long black robes entered the auditorium and sat down. I asked the people backstage who they were and they did not know, but they said the group had attended several meetings on campus and each time had succeeded in breaking up the meeting. The last time was earlier that week when, after 15 minutes of their jeers and shouting, former Vice President Hubert Humphrey walked out in the middle of his speech.

News like this is great for relaxing you just before you perform! We prayed together that God would supernaturally stop the group from doing anything that would hinder His work that night. For the next two hours, they sat there without saying a word or moving. At the end of the program, they got up and quietly filed out. That night scores of students received Christ.

I also remembered various mishaps over the years, such as the time I spoke on the campus in Tampa, Florida. A student's cigarette dropped through the floor and started a fire in some curtain material below. Smoke began coming up around the stage. The aisles and doorways were jammed with an overflow crowd, and I knew people would be hurt or even killed if we announced the fire. Since the audience was not aware of the danger, I continued the program while the fire crew worked below. I explained that the smoke was part of the atmosphere for our presentation. Only after the danger was over did I tell them what had happened.

During another performance in Florida, as I reached the most important part of the program a horrible smell permeated the area. It was so bad I could hardly talk. A small group of radical students had entered the back of the auditorium and thrown a stink bomb into the middle of the audience to try to break up the meeting. However, because of their interest in the message, the audience endured the smell. Not one person left.

Some of the experiences overseas were even more harrowing. In El Salvador I did a program for some top military men.

Two generals were sitting in the front row. In one of my numbers I go into the audience and pull money out of the noses and ears of the people. At this program I picked up the hat of a soldier near the front and poured a number of coins out of it. He was surprised, but I was more surprised because . . . under the hat he was holding a loaded revolver in his hand! Afterward I learned that he was one of the men assigned to keep his eye—and revolver—on me since they didn't know much about me. With two generals in attendance, they weren't taking any chances.

In Liberia I had a performance before the president and about fifty government leaders he had invited. An attempt had been made on his life the week before, so secret service guards were stationed around the stage to watch my every move. One man kept a loaded gun pointed at me offstage—just in case I got too close to the president. Afterward, the president commented over and over that this was the most inspiring talk he had ever heard, and he instructed his personal assistant to tape my presentation at the university the following evening so he could hear it again and refer to it later. We spent another hour talking about the spiritual needs of his country and the world.

Thinking back over all these experiences, I realized that though it was a great privilege to win the Performing Arts Fellowship, the equivalent of an Oscar in the movie profession, no honors could begin to equal the fact that people were resolving their eternal destinies. That was my greatest award. I wondered if I should even attend the banquet. It was scheduled while I was in the middle of another tour. One part of me felt I should not be diverted. Yet this was a unique opportunity to give God the credit for what He had accomplished in my life.

The award would be presented by Mark Wilson at a gala, black-tie event in the Beverly Wilshire. Many outstanding entertainers would attend—magicians such as Doug Henning, David Copperfield and Blackstone; musicians and actors such as Cary Grant, Liberace, Bill Bixby and Bob Barker. I wanted to share with them the significance of this award. I reached over to my desk and took a yellow pad.

"I am very grateful and deeply honored to receive this award," I wrote quickly. "The magicians here tonight who know me personally know that I very sincerely and very strongly believe that God is the One who gives each of us all the talents and abilities we have in this life.

"Through the years my greatest desire has been to honor Him and express my thanks to Him for all He has allowed me to do through the gift that He has given me. So in accepting this award, I not only want to express my thanks to you and to the Academy, but also to Him for who He is, and for allowing me to be involved with you in such an exciting and enjoyable profession."

Assisted by his son Tim, André presents a new magical exercising machine, in which the girl's arms, neck and legs are "stretched."

In his new Easter spectacular, André is about to send three people on a "trip." The basket falls open and the people disappear.

In this scene from the André Kole Christmas production, the girl will be shot through the air into a star on the opposite side of the stage.

Chapter Eleven

REAL POWER

My missionary escorts had warned me that this campus was one of the most anti-American universities in Latin America. In recent weeks several speakers had been attacked and beaten. Two had nearly died.

We arrived at the university in Santiago, Chili, and immediately noticed something was awry. Hundreds of students were milling around and the mood was tense, as if they anticipated a riot. "They're on strike," someone told us. I thought that was a good reason to cancel the performance, but before I could suggest that, someone ran up to us. "They're waiting for you!" he shouted. "There are at least two thousand people!"

Several bodyguards surrounded me and we were quickly escorted to an outdoor theater. The students were standing, surrounding the stage and I immediately observed that I could not easily escape. Bodyguards would be virtually useless against such a mob.

I thought again of the words I had read in Acts a few hours earlier. Paul had experienced severe resistence to his preaching, but God spoke to him one night: "Do not be afraid any longer, but go on speaking and do not be silent; for I am with you, and no man will attack you in order to harm you, for I have many people in this city."[1]

Those words were nearly two thousand years old but they could not have been more relevant. I silently offered a prayer of thanksgiving for that encouragement, and with a surge of confidence I stepped out onto the stage. A chorus of whistles and shouts greeted me, drowning out the emcee's introduction. I reminded myself that this was only a sign of their great hunger and need for God. I silently prayed, "Lord, please draw them to Yourself through Your Holy Spirit."

I quickly noticed a group of young men near the front who appeared to be the ringleaders. I yelled for their leader to come forward to help me, explaining that he was surely the bravest man in the crowd. As he came forward, my Chinese cure for dandruff was rolled out. This contraption, which looks like an ancient guillotine, quieted the crowd slightly, yet the background music still could not be heard. My victim looked skeptically at the apparatus, but was too proud to back away. Kneeling, he inserted his head and hands. The blade descended and appeared to pass through the young man's neck without injuring him.

Without my usual patter between tricks, I got a bucket and began picking coins from the air. Reaching into the first row, I pulled coins from one student's nose, dumped some more from another's hat, and picked more from another's ear.

As I moved quickly through my tricks, the crowd became more quiet. I had been warned that students with rocks, eggs and other objects were stationed in the crowd, waiting to break up the program on a given signal. But nothing happened.

After thirty minutes, the bold, restless crowd had been supernaturally transformed into a quiet audience, spellbound as I began to share the message of Jesus Christ. At the conclusion of the 50-minute program, the students erupted into a long, sustained ovation. Many swarmed onto the stage, wanting to hear more. Others asked for appointments with local staff to talk more about Jesus Christ. It was another hour before we could begin to make our way off campus to another meeting.

As we left, a university administrator expressed amazement at the response and attention from the students. He had never seen any program so well received on the campus. I knew only one way to explain the crowd's transformation—the power of the Holy Spirit.

During my years of performing, God's power has protected me in all kinds of dangerous situations. I have never been injured by any audience. Even more incredible, I have never missed a performance, despite inclement weather, illness and almost impossible travel schedules—as many as a hundred shows in a hundred days in a dozen different countries.

I did not always understand the power of the Holy Spirit. The first three years of my Christian experience were perhaps the toughest years I ever lived through. I was convinced of the reality of Jesus Christ, and that He had accepted my prayer of invitation and had come into my life, but I fell into the trap for which I had criticized others. I became busy in church and religious activities, while finding it almost impossible to live a consistent Christian life each day.

Probably the greatest lesson I have ever learned is that God does not want us to work for Him. He simply wants us to allow Him to do His work in and through us. During those three years of trying to live a good, religious life, I experienced little real joy or happiness. Life was a constant struggle. Then I began to hear about the Holy Spirit. I learned that Jesus Christ, as He finished His ministry on this earth, said He had to go away. "I tell you the truth, it is to your advantage that I go away; for if I do not go away, the Helper [another word for the Holy Spirit] shall not come to you; but if I go, I will send Him to you."[2] In other words, Jesus Christ physically left the earth so that He could be present spiritually within the lives of everyone willing to receive Him. At the very moment a person receives Christ, He enters into that life in the person of the Holy Spirit.

Regarding the Holy Spirit, the testimony of one Bible character particularly impressed me. This man, Simon the Sorcerer, was exceptionally qualified to recognize whether or not Christianity was just a trick. Simon was one of the greatest, if not *the* greatest magician of his time. We read in Acts 8 that he was practicing magic in the city of Samaria, claiming to be someone exceptional. Everyone was giving him attention until Philip began preaching the gospel. As Philip preached, a number of miracles happened, including the healing of several who were lame and paralyzed. Simon was so impressed that he also believed and was baptized.

As I have said, it is easy for an experienced magician to fool scientists, theologians, ministers and priests, because they do not think like magicians, but it is extremely difficult to fool another magician. Simon would not have been easily fooled. Apparently the miracles he saw were greater than anything he'd ever observed.

Then the apostles Peter and John came to town, and as they laid their hands on the believers, the Holy Spirit was manifested. Simon offered money to buy the secret of the apostles' power, but they rebuked him for thinking that he could buy the gift of God with money. He was terrified by the power he saw.

Just what does it mean to be filled with the Holy Spirit? It is something like a picture I saw many years ago of a single piece of straw that was driven through a telephone pole during a tornado. How in the world could a flimsy blade of grass go clear through a pole? It could not in its own strength, but the power of the tornado drove it through the pole. Likewise, we are weak until we are willing to surrender to the power of the Holy Spirit. Only then can we experience supernatural power.

In John 15, Jesus used the analogy of the vine and branches to explain what it means to be filled with the Spirit. Today He might use an illustration of electricity and the light bulb. No matter how hard a light bulb tries to shine in its own power, it cannot succeed. The only way it can shine is to surrender itself to the power of the electric current. Perhaps Jesus would say something like this:

"I am the electricity, you are the light bulbs, and My Father is the electrician. Abide in Me as I abide in you. Just as the light bulb cannot produce light unless it abides in the electricity, so neither can you unless you abide in Me. I am the electricity, you are the light bulbs. He who abides in Me and I in him sheds much light. Apart from Me you can do absolutely nothing. If you abide in Me and My words abide in you, ask whatever you wish and it shall be done for you. By this is My Father glorified and illuminated, that ye shed much light and in so doing prove to be My disciples."

We experience the power of the Holy Spirit by surrendering to Him by faith. The Bible commands Christians to be filled with the Holy Spirit. It also promises that if we ask anything according to God's will, He hears us and grants our requests.[3] So we can be filled with the Holy Spirit through prayer—an expression of our faith. We can invite God, through the Holy Spirit, to take control of our lives.

I do a number of illusions with light bulbs to illustrate how the Holy Spirit works. One illustration incorporates three bulbs of different sizes: One is 200 watts, another is 50, and the third is only 2 1/2 watts. I use these to illustrate how God gives each of us different talents. Becoming jealous of another person who may have more talent is a great danger. So is feeling superior to someone with less talent. Just as each light bulb was created for a different purpose, so are we. The 200-watt bulb does not make a good night light, but the 2 1/2-watt bulb does. They have different functions. And no light bulb will work without the power of electricity flowing through it. If the 200-watt bulb thinks that because it is so much brighter, it doesn't need electricity, it will become useless.

I found out how true this is in my life when I did four programs in one day on a midwest campus. I had performed and given my Christian testimony for several years and had always seen people respond by giving their lives to Jesus Christ. On that day, however, I had a tremendous audience at the first program, but no spiritual response. At the second performance, the same thing happened. I couldn't understand what was wrong. At the third program, the audience was again very warm and receptive, but not a single person indicated that he had received Christ.

I spent an hour alone before the final program, searching my heart to see what was wrong. As I grew silent before God, I realized that a certain thought had crept into my thinking. It was the idea that if a person just learned to do what I did and to say what I said, he automatically would see the same type of spiritual response. The outcome did not really depend on God; it was just a matter of doing the tricks and saying the words.

God used those three shows to demonstrate that without the power of the Holy Spirit, I could do nothing. I confessed my wrong attitude and thanked Him for showing me this truth. I asked Him to again do His work through me. That night, I gave the same program, but saw different results. Sixteen students indicated they received Christ. To my knowledge, from that day on every single program I have done has had a spiritual response from the audience. Sometimes the response has been in the hundreds, but I cannot take credit for that. The Holy Spirit, working through me, is responsible for every conversion.

I also use light bulbs to illustrate the problem Christians have with sin. That battle confuses many people; they can't understand why they continue to want to sin. When we receive Christ, however, we do not lose the old sin nature with which we all are born. Instead we receive a new nature.

117

I illustrate this with two light bulbs mounted on a "Y" shaped socket. The little, dark, ugly bulb represents the old nature; the bright light bulb represents the new nature. I tie ropes to each bulb, symbolizing the fact that our old nature is tied to Satan, our new nature to God. Satan constantly tries to tempt us, while God tries to communicate His life to us through the Holy Spirit.

Thousands of Christians throughout the world live in defeat because they listen to the wrong voice. They listen to Satan rather than God. Whichever voice we give our attention to will dominate our lives. It's like the story of the Indian who said two dogs were fighting inside him—a black dog and a white dog. When he was asked which dog was winning, he answered, "The one I feed the most." *The secret to growing in the Christian life is to feed our new nature while starving the old.* We can do this through consciously day-by-day studying the Scriptures, fellowshiping with other believers, witnessing for our faith, and praying.

I have seen the power of the Holy Spirit at work in innumerable ways. One is the fact that I speak before thousands of people each year, and millions more on television. It certainly is not my nature to be a speaker. I am very shy and quiet, and content to be alone for long periods of time. But God has given me a tremendous desire to share what I have discovered, and to explain to others how they can experience the same joy and excitement in their lives.

The Holy Spirit was the only reason I could go out before dangerous, unruly crowds in Latin America, knowing I easily could be killed. The reality of Christ overcomes my fear of death, and I am confident that I am safest while in God's will. Many times I have stood before antagonistic crowds which had been whipped to a fervor by Marxist students, and each time I have seen God's Spirit change that crowd so that by the time I started sharing the message of Christ, they were completely silent and attentive.

The only way I can explain this is with the words of the apostle Paul: "I was with you in weakness and in fear and in much trembling. And my message and my preaching were not in persuasive words of wisdom, but in demonstration of the Spirit and of power."[4] I am convinced that, as Christians, we have tremendous potential. We can accomplish *anything*, if we're empowered by the Holy Spirit. God has given each one of us unique talents, but we can utilize them only through His power. With His Spirit, our lives reflect a dramatically different lifestyle that is evident to those around us—a difference that is even worth dying for.

As Bill Bright has said, "The dedicated Spirit-filled Christian life is not an easy life, but it is a life filled with adventure and thrills, the likes of which one cannot possibly experience in any other way. Whether or not we're Christians, we are going to have problems in this life. Christians or not, we will one day die. If I am going to be a Christian at all, I want all that God has for me, and I want to be all that He wants me to be. If I am to suffer at all and one day die, why not suffer and die for the highest and best, for the Lord Jesus Christ and His gospel?"

The potential of the Spirit-filled Christian life is dramatically illustrated through the story of the forty singing wrestlers. In the days when the ruling passion of the Roman Emperor Nero was the extermination of the Christians, he had a band of soldiers known as the "Emperor's Wrestlers." These men were the best and bravest of the land. In the great amphitheater they upheld the arms of the emperor against all challengers. Before each contest they stood before the emperor's throne and cried, "We, the wrestlers, wrestling for thee, O Emperor, to win for thee the victory and from thee the victor's crown."

When the great Roman army was sent to fight in faraway Gaul, no soldiers were braver or more loyal than this band of wrestlers led by their centurian, Vespasian. But news reached Nero that many had accepted the Christian faith.

To be a Christian meant death, even to those who served Nero best. Therefore this decree was straightway dispatched to Vespasian: "If there be any among the soldiers who cling to the faith of the Christian, they must die." He received the decree in the dead of winter, while the soldiers were camped on the shore of a frozen inland lake. The winter had been hard, but enduring the many hardships together united them more closely.

Vespasian's heart sank as he read the emperor's message. He called the soldiers together and asked, "Are there any among you who cling to the faith of the Christian? If so, let him step forward."

Forty wrestlers instantly stepped forward two paces, respectfully saluted and stood at attention. Vespasian paused. He had not expected so many. "The decree has come from your emperor," he said, "that any who cling to the faith of the Christian must die. For the sake of your country, your comrades, your loved ones, renounce this false faith." Not one of the forty moved.

Vespasian pleaded with them long and earnestly without prevailing upon a single man to deny his Lord. Finally he said, "The decree of the emperor must be obeyed, but I am not willing that your blood be on your comrades. I am going to order that you march out upon the lake of ice and I shall leave you there to the mercy of the elements. Fires, however, will be waiting here on the shore to welcome any willing to renounce this false faith."

At sundown, the forty wrestlers were stripped of all their clothing. Without a word they turned and, falling into columns of four, marched onto the lake of ice. As they marched, they broke into chorus with the old chant of the arena: "Forty wrestlers, wrestling for Thee, O Christ, to win for Thee the victory and from Thee, the Victor's crown."

Through the long hours of the night, Vespasian stood by his campfire and waited. The words of the wrestlers' song became fainter and fainter. As morning drew near, one figure, overcome by exposure, crept quietly toward the fire. In the extremity of his suffering he had renounced his Lord. Then faintly but clearly from out of the darkness came the song, "Thirty-nine wrestlers, wrestling for Thee, O Christ, to win for Thee the victory and from Thee, the Victor's crown."

Vespasian looked at the figure drawing close to the fire, then out toward the frozen lake. Who can say, but perhaps he saw the greater light shining there in the darkness. Off came his helmet, down went his shield, and he sprang onto the ice crying, "Forty wrestlers, wrestling for Thee, O Christ, to win for Thee the victory and from Thee, the Victor's crown."

The number of God's forty singing wrestlers was complete.

Chapter Twelve

IS PRAYER MAGIC?

Is prayer magic? That question was asked in a magazine article. It's a fair question, for many people repeat certain prayers as a religious ritual hoping for some magical effect. Some try prayer only when all else fails.

One reason that people find prayer unfulfilling is that they don't understand what it really is. When my children were small, it occurred to me that I could hypnotize Robyn and Tim and make them do almost anything I wanted. I could tell them to stand up, sit down, eat their spinach, and they'd do those things. I could tell them, "I want you to tell me 'I love you,' " and they would say, "I love you." But it would mean nothing to me because they'd only be doing what I had commanded them to do.

One afternoon I was working in my office and Robyn was running around the room, making a lot of noise. I asked her to leave so I could concentrate. "I don't want to leave, Daddy," she said. "I'll just sit here and be quiet." She sat down near me, but I figured she couldn't keep quiet for long. "Why don't you go out and play with Timothy?" "No Daddy," she answered, "I just want to be with you."

When she said that, I gave her a big hug. She responded and said, "I love my daddy." And I said, "I love my Robyn."

In that moment I learned more about prayer and God's love than I could by reading a dozen books on theology and religion. God desires our fellowship, but He doesn't force us to communicate with Him. He gives us a free will to express our love to Him, or to reject His love. Robyn helped me see that prayer is a voluntary relationship with our heavenly Father.

A few years ago I heard about a big rugged construction worker named Joe. Joe was very quiet, but all the men liked him, and they knew he had a very strong faith in God. Every day during lunch break he went into the chapel to pray. One day one of the men asked him, "What do you say to God when you go and pray?" Joe answered, "I just say, 'Jesus, this is Joe.' "

Sometime later, Joe was hospitalized from an accident. His fellow workers visited him, but he couldn't talk and part of his face was bandaged because of the injuries. They all noticed, however, a tremendous expression of peace on his face despite the pain. Later, after Joe recovered, one of the men asked him, "How could you endure such pain and still have such a peaceful look while you were in the hospital?" Joe answered, "During the time I was lying there, I kept hearing the words, 'Joe, this is Jesus.' "

That story explains prayer as well as any I've heard. Often we think prayer consists of long sentences and many words. In reality, it may just be the awareness of God—sitting in His presence and enjoying Him. I especially like the following definition: *Prayer is simply a conversation between two people who love each other.* So often people feel they need to do all the talking in prayer, but genuine prayer also allows God time to speak to us through His Holy Spirit.

The author of the article I referred to at the start of this chapter summarized this concept well:

> Prayer is not magic. It is a relationship with God in an intimate, ongoing relationship of love, where we may express our adoration of Him as a person and our God. It is where we can safely express ourselves in the depth of whom we are, confessing our sins and accepting His forgiveness. Prayer is where we seek God's support in our vulnerability and needs, and lastly, where we ask for His help and encouragement in our lives, relationships, and work, by His will and His love for us. To engage in prayer as magic is to reject the autonomous holy person, God. To engage in prayer as relationship is to be vulnerable, and to trust God's goodness and wisdom.[1]

The beauty of such a relationship is that we can pray anytime, anywhere, about anything. The apostle Paul wrote that we should "pray without ceasing."[2] To me, that means we should enjoy God's presence at all times, not just go to Him when we are in need.

But I find that I also need some time each day to be totally alone with God, so in solitude I kneel and pray. (Kneeling is not necessary for prayer; it simply helps me reflect my heart attitude toward God.) During these times, I can concentrate solely on Him and bring to Him my concerns.

A young man who was desperately seeking God sought out a wise old man who lived in a nearby beach house. He asked him, "Old man, how can I see God?"

The old man obviously knew God and had a depth which few of us ever experience. He pondered for what seemed to be a very long time, then finally responded quietly, "Young man, I am not sure that I can really help you. You see, I have a very different problem from yours. I cannot *not* see Him." Prayer means involving God and seeing His hand in anything and everything.

Perhaps the part of prayer most important to me is praise. That's when I tell God how wonderful He is and reflect on His attributes. Reading through the psalms and even praying some of them back to God helps me do this.

Praise is important because it increases our confidence in God, which is the key to answered prayer. The more we pray and believe God, the more we see Him answer our prayers, and the more confidence we have in Him. This is illustrated in a story about a church in a Kansas farming community that was concerned about a severe drought. The problem was so serious that one Sunday the members agreed to return to the church after lunch to pray for rain.

As one man walked to church that afternoon, he met a little boy carrying an umbrella. "Where are you going with the umbrella?" he asked.

"Haven't you heard?" the boy answered. "We're going to pray for rain today."

The man smiled as they walked to church together. After the prayer meeting, the man enjoyed sharing the little boy's umbrella as they walked home in the rain.

So many times we pray without really believing God hears us and will answer. Yet He is the God who created the heavens and the earth; He controls the wind and the waves and the rain. A God that powerful is a God I can believe will hear and respond.

That doesn't mean God always answers my prayers the way I intended. I mentioned that I have never missed a scheduled performance in all my years of traveling, but I did almost miss one. I was in Sri Lanka (when it used to be called Ceylon) and had a program scheduled the next day in Singapore. There were only three flights a week to Singapore, and the one I was scheduled to take was running 24 hours behind schedule. So I phoned ahead to tell the university staff that I would not make the show. They rescheduled the program for the next day.

They had built a special outdoor stage for my show and prayed that it would not rain. The weather was fine on the day it originally was scheduled, but as I arrived in Singapore, the storm clouds were moving in. By show time it was raining too hard to hold the program outside, so hundreds of people crowded into a small auditorium. As we saw people being turned away, we wondered why this was the first program I had missed, and why God had prevented us from having that program outside where more people could enjoy it. After the show we learned that the outdoor stage had collapsed. If we had used that stage, several people would have been seriously injured and perhaps even killed.

I have found that God is equally concerned about little things as He is the large things. No circumstance is too small for Him. Once while I was in California, I was scheduled to meet with Bill Bright at Campus Crusade for Christ's international headquarters. As I entered his office, I heard him ask his secretary, "Have you prayed about this?" Embarrassed, she said, "No, I haven't." He responded, "Why don't we pray that God will help us find this tape."

A minute later the secretary returned and explained to me that she was having a hard time finding a tape by a certain speaker. I told her, "Arlis Priest in Arizona has that tape." I was probably the only one out of hundreds of people at headquarters who knew where that tape was. A coincidence? Because I have seen many such prayers answered over the years, I believe that God brought me into the office at that precise moment to serve as the answer to that prayer.

During the early years of my ministry, I needed a trailer to use on our tours, as we were traveling with small children. But we didn't have much money and trailers were expensive. We prayed about it as a family, and then I visited a dealer.

When I told the man what I needed, he showed me a trailer

that fit our needs perfectly. "This trailer has been on the lot for months and I haven't been able to sell it. I don't know why it hasn't moved. Maybe God was reserving it for you." He thought for a moment, then said, "Why don't you take this trailer and use it as long as you need. I won't charge you for it. Just bring it back when you're finished."

That was another experience that strengthened my confidence in God. Over and over again I have seen that faith is like a muscle, and prayer is the exercise that helps it grow. Bill Bright told me that when he started his ministry in 1951, he prayed that one person would come to Christ. When God answered that prayer, Dr. Bright prayed for a dozen converts. As God answered that, his vision grew. He prayed for hundreds of conversions through the ministry of Campus Crusade for Christ, then thousands, then millions. All of those prayers have been answered and now he is believing God for more than a billion people throughout the world to come to Christ.

My faith began to grow when, as a young boy, I was in an orange grove one day. The fruit wasn't ripe yet, but I was thirsty and craved an orange. My friend suggested I pray. I did not know Christ yet, but I prayed. Then I walked over two rows, looked up into a tree and saw a beautiful ripe orange. I believe God answered that prayer to show me that He is real.

In the early '60s, I prayed for an opportunity to perform and speak at university fraternities and sororities to present Jesus Christ. When I saw the response at those meetings, I began praying for larger, campus-wide meetings. Soon I was speaking before groups of more than a thousand students. Then I began praying for a way to further expand my ministry. God provided the opportunity to make two films, which have been shown to millions throughout the world.

As I have observed God's faithfulness, my faith has increased. For several years I've prayed about producing the world's largest stage show, during which I would recreate some of the great miracles of the Bible. God has started to answer that prayer through special Christmas and Easter shows, and I anticipate the day when the full dream will be realized.

I find it exciting to be in situations where my only hope is to trust God, such as my most recent trip through India, which was during the Monsoon season. Because of the anticipated size of the audiences, all except one of the programs were scheduled to be outdoors. I was to visit seven cities in seven days, but it seemed impossible to avoid being rained out of several shows.

Together with the national staff, we prayed that God would allow all seven of the programs to go as scheduled. In every city the weather cleared as we arrived. At all our outdoor performances, we had overflow crowds and no rain. And as we left the city, the rains returned. The one exception was the show we scheduled indoors. A group of Marxist students protested outside, trying to break up the program. They disturbed us to the point that we were afraid the confusion might disperse the crowd. On stage I silently prayed that God would supernaturally intervene so we could continue. As soon as I had prayed, I heard a crash of thunder and a torrential downpour. The radicals quickly fled, allowing us to proceed without further interruption.

As I've traveled throughout the world, I have had opportunities to speak to people of many different religions. Sometimes, in situations where crowds were almost 100 percent non-Christian, I have been tempted to dilute my message. But God always has demonstrated His power in answer to prayer.

On my first tour in Asia, I performed for a Hindu and Muslim audience in Madras, India's fourth largest city. Invitations had been sent to the city leaders for this special appearance, in which the mayor had agreed to preside. Despite the temptation to water down the message, I proceeded with my normal program. At the end, the mayor—a very devout Muslim—came on stage and took the microphone. For a moment, I thought he was going to denounce what I said. But to my amazement and that of many others, he told of the problems of India and said he felt the message he had just heard was the answer to that country's problems.

Another time I appeared at a college in Pakistan. Nearly a thousand students squeezed into the auditorium, and of those, 95 percent were Muslim. My custom in every show is to tell the audience that after a break I will explain how a person can come into a personal relationship with Jesus Christ. I encourage those who are not interested to leave. The Christians responsible for arranging this meeting advised me not to do this, as they feared that everyone would leave. But we took the ten minute break, and only three people left. I later found out that the three who left were Christians, and they later returned. All the Muslim students stayed and their interest and attention was phenomenal. That further proved to me that if God is knowable, people want to know Him.

If you doubt that God hears or answers prayer, I challenge you to put God to the test. I think God may answer some prayers of a non-believer, but it's like asking a neighbor to do something for you in an emergency, as opposed to asking a close member of your own family. You can be certain, however, that He will hear one prayer—your cry for forgiveness, and the receiving of God's Son, Jesus Christ, into your life. Once you become a Christian, God becomes your Father; a loving Father who wants to provide for His children.

If you are a Christian and you don't see God answering prayer, I encourage you to keep a small notebook and record your requests and God's answers. He may not respond in the way you ask. But He will answer. Keeping a journal of His answers is one of the best ways to develop confidence in God.

Most important, remember that prayer is not asking for things, but a relationship. God loves us, and He wants us to enjoy His presence through prayer.

André Kole and his wife Kathy.

Chapter Thirteen

THE ULTIMATE TEST

In a time when many marriages are disintegrating, I have been privileged to experience not one, but two wonderful marriages. My first wife, of twenty years, went to be with the Lord in 1976. One year later, God brought Kathy into my life, and later we were married. She was not a replacement of Aljeana, but God's perfect provision for both of our needs.

We have talked about reality as opposed to illusion. In my presentations, I always try to dispel the illusion that becoming a Christian eliminates all problems. In fact, only when we are confronted with pain, suffering and death is the reality of our faith tested.

According to the latest statistics, the death rate for every hundred people is still 100 percent. The Bible says, "It is appointed for men to die once."[1] Everyone has an appointment. For some, it is a few years earlier than for others. For Aljeana, it was November 28, 1976, at the age of thirty-eight.

I first met Aljeana in grade school, when she started to assist me in some of my shows. The main purpose of an assistant is to make the magician look good. Aljeana was perfect in that respect—very attractive with good stage presence, plus she was small and agile and just right for some of our unusual illusions. Over the years, we developed a oneness of feeling and timing so that we knew what each other was thinking on stage without speaking. She could anticipate any problems and help me out of a jam.

We married while I was in college. Aljeana, with her sweet spirit, was committed to my career in magic to the extent that she was willing to sacrifice her own desires in order to help acquire some of the very expensive equipment we needed. We labored together toward the same goals, intent on making our lives count for eternity.

In December, 1974, Aljeana was Christmas shopping with

our two children, Robyn and Tim, when suddenly she experienced a strange dizziness and had to be helped to a chair. The feeling passed in a few minutes, but during the holidays it occurred several more times.

After consulting our doctors, we learned that she had an incurable brain tumor. In layman's language the doctors said she had a time bomb in her head that could go off at any moment. Eventually they would have to operate, but that would only prolong her life for a short time; it would not cure the problem. They advised us that if we wanted to do anything or take any trip, we had better do it soon.

Aljeana and I talked and prayed about what we should do. For more than a decade we had traveled throughout the world, sharing our discovery about the reality of Christ with millions of people through our TV shows, films and personal appearances. We both concluded that we would continue working together as long as possible.

We shared the news of Aljeana's condition with our children and explained that their mother might go to heaven soon. Then we talked about the fact that everyone in the world is infected with a sickness far worse than Aljeana's—the disease the Bible calls sin. This disease not only would kill a person physically, but also could cause one to be separated from God forever. We explained that even though there was no known medical cure for Aljeana's problem, there is a cure for the disease of sin. So as long as we could, we wanted to keep telling people how they could know this cure, Jesus Christ, in a personal way.

During the two years leading up to Aljeana's departure, God taught us many great lessons about life and the exciting adventure of death. He gave each of us supernatural peace and joy beyond our human understanding or ability to express. The prayers of many friends from around the world strengthened us and our trust in God freed us of any worry, anxiety or fear.

While Aljeana still could do some speaking, she always shared a poem that ended with these lines: "We would not long for heaven, if earth held our only joy." In the last weeks of Aljeana's suffering, she experienced a great longing and anticipation of heaven. The Bible says, "Let heaven fill your thoughts; don't spend your time worrying about things down here."[2] We found that the more we know about heaven, the less important this life seems to be, including its suffering.

Another source of power and victory during this ordeal came from our time of praising the Lord. As long as Aljeana could read the Bible, she spent about 90 percent of her time in the psalms. There she gained comfort and strength for every phase of her experience.

As the illness progressed, her suffering increased. Gradually she began to lose the ability to do anything for herself. She lost the use of her arms and legs. She could not move her head or body. She became totally blind. Others had to move her, bathe her, feed her (when she could eat) and care for her every need. After her brain surgery and radiation treatments, she lost her hair. Day after day she could do nothing but lie in bed.

Yet not once did I hear her complain. On the contrary, many times she said, "Thank You, Lord, for the pain." One day while a friend was sitting quietly with her, she noticed a smile on Aljeana's face. "Aljeana, what are you smiling about?" she asked. "Oh, God is so good to me," she replied.

God heals all of his children; sometimes in this life, sometimes in the life to come. Some people did not understand why God did not heal Aljeana in this life. I believe that God chose her for a very special and important task: to demonstrate His ability to impart supernatural strength in the midst of pain, suffering and death.

I, too, experienced this sustenance. In my eyes, Aljeana was the most attractive and lovely person I had ever known, but as her illness progressed, her physical beauty diminished. Yet my love for her did not. Instead, it grew and deepened. The inner beauty that radiated through her far surpassed any physical beauty she ever had. I experienced a God-given, supernatural love far beyond the deep, wonderful love I had known for her when she was in good health.

The time came when it looked as though Aljeana would die soon. For several days she was in a coma and the doctor said she could expire at any moment. With my permission, he tried one last bit of surgery. As a result, she made a remarkable recovery for a few days.

When she came out of the coma, one of the first things Aljeana said was, "Who was the man who was with me all the time?" She explained that a young man stood by her bed and never left her during the critical days through which she had just come.

In her words, "He seemed to have a special feeling for me, and when the pain was very bad, he held my hand and comforted me. I don't think I could have made it without him." When I asked if he was still there, she said, "No, he left yesterday morning,"—the time when she began to recover. That day we received in the mail a card with the Bible verse, "The Lord stood with me, and strengthed me."[3]

I hesitate to jump to any conclusions concerning this experience, but I often have wondered if God allowed Aljeana to return to us so we could know the extent of His care for us when we come to our final hours. The Bible says, "His loved ones are very precious to Him and He does not lightly let them die."[4] The Bible also teaches that, when we die, the angels will carry us into the presence of God.[5]

Aljeana didn't want to talk more about her experience. A few weeks later, however, her life once again began to fade. I had mixed emotions when she quietly said to us one night, "That young man has come back and I am glad he is here." Shortly thereafter she lost consciousness and never recovered.

One of the greatest lessons God taught me through my wife's death concerns our transition from earth to heaven. I illustrated this at her memorial service through the use of two large light bulbs. One represents our present, earthly bodies; the other our heavenly bodies.

The Bible tells us, "For we know that when this tent we live in now is taken down—when we die and leave these bodies—we will have wonderful new bodies in heaven, homes that will be ours forevermore, made for us by God Himself, and not by human hands."[6] A few verses later it says, "Every moment we spend in these earthly bodies is time spent away from our eternal home in heaven with Jesus."[7] As long as we are on earth, the light is on in our earthly bodies. "This precious treasure—this light and power that now shine within us—is held in a perishable container, that is, in our weak bodies."[8]

In the last weeks before Aljeana left her earthly body, she seemed to be in a twilight zone between earth and heaven. A couple of times she seemed to be getting better, and I saw her grow brighter here again. Then as her life began to fade and grow dimmer here, I pictured her growing brighter and brighter in heaven.

On the final night of Aljeana's earthly life, my brother, his wife and I entered her hospital room together. She had not responded to anything that day. We noticed the long pauses between each breath, and my brother started counting the seconds between breaths. We counted twenty seconds. Then thirty seconds. Then forty seconds. Then there was no more. We had just witnessed her last breath. After thirty-eight years, Aljeana's light here had gone out. She was released into total healing, free to begin her new life in heaven.

The visual illustration of lights was a tremendous comfort to me because when the night came for her light to go out completely here, I already was thinking of her as being more in heaven. This made the transition easier for me. It is tragic that many people think of their loved ones who have died as being in a coffin. Not once have I thought of Aljeana as being anywhere but in heaven with Jesus. All that remains in that fancy box is what the Bible calls "the perishable container." It also says that to be absent from the body is to be present with the Lord.[9] Today, Aljeana is alive in heaven, and her light is

André often uses magical illustrations to communicate spiritual truths. Here he uses a light bulb to demonstrate the spiritual dimension of man.

shining brighter than ever.

A Christian's death is a time of sorrow for loved ones because of the temporary separation. But it also is a time of joy and celebration as we rejoice with the believer in his new life and home in heaven. Because of this, my family and I planned a very special service of thanksgiving and praise for Aljeana's life here and her new life in heaven.

Aljeana and I had agreed that we did not want the slow, depressing organ music usually associated with a funeral. This was her heavenly coronation, and we thought the music should be in keeping with the celebration. By waiting a week, we had time to arrange an unusual service, which included a singing group and orchestra.

The memorial service was important, but even more important to me was the time I took to be alone with my thoughts and memories. I prayed alone, wept alone and allowed God to minister to me alone in my grief. This was the greatest and most precious religious experience of my life.

Some people wanted to do me a favor by not giving me time to think, but that would have cheated me out of an important experience. I was very jealous of this time and guarded it carefully. Probably at very few times in my life will God's Word and presence mean as much to me. I soaked up His presence, allowing Him to love and comfort me.

Another source of blessing was the cards and letters so many people sent. I took the time to read and meditate on each one. One of the most comforting and meaningful thoughts I received was: "If Aljeana is with Jesus, and Jesus is with me, then Aljeana cannot be far away."

During my three intensive days alone with God, I confronted and dealt with the sorrow of losing my wife. Then I realized that life had to go on. I would face times of sadness from our separation. Various memories would remind me of my loneliness. Yet, I did not want to dwell in the past. I had work to do. I had new dreams for a major stage show that would recreate some of the miracles of the Bible. I wanted to dramatize the story of Shadrach, Meshach and Abednego in the fiery furnace, Moses leading the Israelites through the Red Sea, Ezekiel's dream in which the valley of dry bones becomes a nation, Jesus walking on the water and the resurrection of Christ. I wanted people to experience in a small way the greatness of my God.

Early in 1977 God brought Kathy into my life. Some mutual friends arranged our meeting at the Tucson airport on my way home from Los Angeles. It was hard to imagine that I could fall in love again, yet that night I almost missed my flight to Phoenix, and driving home I got lost twice in an area where I'd lived for years.

Until I met Kathy, I had given little thought to the possibility of remarriage. For one thing, I figured it would be almost impossible to find someone who would fit into my unusual lifestyle. I had at least seven prerequisites: She would have to be a Christian. She would have to be interested in my work. She would have to endure my extensive traveling. Because of the pace of my life, she probably would have to be younger than me. She would have to love my two teenage children. She would have to be satisfied to not have any more children. Finally, I did not want her to fall in love with André Kole, the showman, but with the real me. The chances of one woman meeting all seven requirements seemed remote.

It was not my normal character to move quickly into a romantic relationship. In fact, I had avoided every situation where someone had tried to match me with a girl. Yet soon after we met, Kathy and I felt God's leading so strongly that we didn't want to waste any time. I often have told her that if I did not believe in God for any other reason, I would have to believe in Him because of her.

We were married on August 10, 1977, and God has continued His perfect plan for our lives. Without her, I am convinced that I would have had to greatly reduce my workload for the sake of my children. Instead, the ministry has flourished. Together, we look forward to many years of service to God.

Chapter Fourteen

FAITH HEALING VERSUS DIVINE HEALING

The service was under way as I slipped into the back of the packed auditorium and glanced around, looking for a seat. Finding none, I moved toward a group of people in wheelchairs and stood among them to observe.

The audience eagerly listened to the 200-voice choir which was accompanied by a five-piece band. Some patients tried to keep time with their feet or hands. One child was attached to an intravenous tube that hung from a pole on his chair. A quadriplegic had a motor-driven chair he controlled with a lever in the palm of his right hand. Another patient, in the advanced stages of multiple sclerosis, leaned over far to one side. All of them had a look of expectation that this night would mark their return to health.

After enthusiastic singing by the congregation, an offertory and a rousing solo by a young gospel singer, the evangelist/faith healer came on stage. "God wants to do a miracle in your life tonight," he said. The more than three thousand people present applauded. "God is in the miracle-working business. If you're here tonight and you have problems with your finances, God wants to heal your finances. If you're here because of problems in your marriage, God wants to heal your marriage. And if you're here tonight because you are sick physically, I am here to tell you that *God wants to heal you.*"

The crowd was ecstatic with those words. Some raised their hands and shouted "Praise God" and "Hallelujah." Others leaned forward in their seats to catch every word. The evangelist held a well-worn Bible in his hands and spoke confidently about miracles it recorded. He said that across the country today, whenever he spoke, he saw God perform miracles just as He had in the time of Christ. And tonight, some people with cancer were going to be healed. Others who suffered chronic back pain were going to be cured. "I do not heal anyone,"

137

he emphasized. "It is the Holy Spirit who heals."

When he finished preaching, the evangelist invited all who desired healing to go into the aisles that surrounded the auditorium. Workers would pray for them there and anoint them with oil. For nearly an hour, the auditorium hummed with prayer and counseling.

Finally the crowd began to thin. Many left rejoicing in the great work God had done in their lives. Others left with tears in their eyes as they pushed away their crippled children. The faces that only an hour ago had shone with anticipation now betrayed a deep and bitter dejection. They had come hoping for a miracle, but God had let them down.

Why can some people give dramatic testimonies about God's healing, while others are left wondering if God even heard their prayers? Many friends fervently prayed that my first wife would be healed, yet despite our faith, she died. Is God playing a lottery game in which only those with the lucky combinations win?

I believe that much of the confusion in this area stems from a misunderstanding of faith healing as opposed to divine healing. Let me define the two.

Faith healing means a person is relieved of symptoms or healed because of his faith. The object of a person's faith may be God, a doctor, a faith healer, a psychic surgeon, even a witch doctor. Miraculous faith cures certainly are not confined to Christianity; they occur in various cultural and religious settings throughout the world. Putting faith in someone—no matter who—can have positive effects on certain diseases, because that is how God has created us. But even the most charismatic healers can never cure some injuries and diseases. Dr. William Nolen explains:

> Patients that go to a ... service, paralyzed from the waist down as the result of injury to the spinal cord, never have been and never will be cured through the ministrations of [the faith-healer/evangelist] .... The patient who suddenly discovers ... that he can now move an arm or a leg that was previously paralyzed had that paralysis as a result of an emotional, not a physical disturbance. Neurotics and hysterics will frequently be relieved of their symptoms by the suggestions and ministrations of charismatic healers.

It is in treating patients of this sort that healers claim their most dramatic triumphs.

There is nothing miraculous about these cures. Psychiatrists, internists, G.P.s, any M.D. who does psychiatric therapy, relieve thousands of such patients of their symptoms every year. Psychotherapy, in which suggestion plays a significant role, is just one of the many tools with which physicians work.[1]

A good doctor uses the principles of faith (sometimes called the placebo effect) to his advantage. He may prescribe sugar pills to help a patient believe he is getting helpful medicine. He may use suggestions like, "You should start feeling better in two days." It is not unethical if it really will help a person recover.

Nolen states that half of the patients who go to a general practitioner will improve even if they do nothing. Another 20 percent often can be helped through suggestion. That means a cure rate of 70 percent, which helps explain the successes of faith healing. After his investigation of faith healing, Nolen also arrived at an explanation for its popularity:

I've gotten a better understanding of why intelligent, rational people go to healers. They go to healers because, for one reason or another, the medical profession has let them down.

Sometimes we doctors let our patients down because, quite simply, we have nothing curative to offer. For example, we don't as yet know how to cure multiple sclerosis, widespread cancer or congenital brain disorders. We explain to patients with these diseases that we are truly sorry but we can't help them. No matter how nicely we do this, no matter how logically we explain that no one else, to our knowledge, can help them either, patients sometimes refuse to accept this bad news.

A second reason people go to healers . . . is that some healers offer patients more warmth and compassion than physicians do. Sure, we pass our pills and perform operations, but do we really care about the people we treat? . . .

A third reason why patients go to healers is that healers do, in fact, help them . . . .We doctors have in the past made the mistake of "putting down" the healers as though they, and those who patronized them, were idiots beneath our contempt. This has been a serious error.[2]

The danger is that most faith healers don't know when to stop. They cannot recognize those disorders that have no psychosomatic cause and will not respond without proper medical attention. For these people a visit to a faith healer can be tragic.

How does divine healing differ from faith healing? *Divine healing is God supernaturally reaching down and miraculously healing a person.* His healing is instantaneous and complete.

An example of divine healing comes from a midwestern pastor who told me about how he was severely burned in an accident when he was a boy. As he was rushed to the hospital, his parents prayed for him. When nurses unwrapped him at the hospital, the burns were gone. As a result, he received Christ and later entered full-time ministry.

Many others have experienced divine healing, but it probably represents only about 5 percent of what people claim are miraculous healings.

How can we distinguish God's hand in healing? And why are some healed while others, who are equally sincere in their belief, have their prayers for healing go unanswered? Confusion in this area causes many to doubt the reality of God, so it is important to understand a few principles.

First, *God is not required to perform in a theatrical setting.* He will work in His own manner, for His own purposes, free from anyone's manipulations.

One respected leader of a charismatic denomination told me that the greatest problem in his churches is "the temptations of pastors to manipulate the emotions of the crowd. People want to see sensational things, so pastors feel they have to cause sensational things to happen in each service."

A few healers actually have resorted to dishonest methods to gain a following. Two nationally known healers induced "slaying in the spirit"—a person falling backward, unconscious, because of the tremendous power of the Holy Spirit—by touching a pressure point in the neck. Another whacks people's foreheads so hard with the heel of his hand that they have little choice but to fall back.

Several healers use cold reading techniques, either consciously or unconsciously. They begin with general statements such as "I believe God wants to heal those of you here tonight who have bad backs." Or, "Someone here just found out he has cancer. God wants to heal you tonight." These men subtly manipulate a crowd, and a few favorable responses cause others to get caught up in the enthusiasm.

One can learn to be a faith healer, as was evidenced by Marjoe Gortner, the famous child evangelist. Steven Gaines writes in his biography:

> In an effort to boost the family's falling income, Marge decided to have Marjoe learn more about the lucrative art of faith healing. She took him to watch the greatest faith healers of the time, the three Kirkwood Brothers . . . .
>
> Marjoe's healing methods were less violent, but every bit as dramatic. His first healings were simplistic: aches and pains that were cured by the firm pressure of his hands on the sufferer's body. While Kirkwood frightened people into recovering, Marjoe turned healing into a mystical experience. People arrived at his meetings already possessed of profound faith. They were prepared to be healed and when they saw the boy, who was clearly an instrument of God, their faith was so intensified that Marjoe had only to touch them to cure a variety of ailments.[3]

Faith or positive thinking may relieve some symptoms for a few days, but eventually the problems recur. God's healing, however, is total and complete, and He can touch a person anytime—He doesn't require the crowd psychology of a healing service to do his work.

Faith healers like to use the excuse "You lack faith" when a person is not healed. That takes the healer off the hook. But God doesn't need excuses. Our lack of faith never negates His power. He can heal us even if we do not believe. Does that mean we don't need faith? No, the Bible clearly teaches that we need to exercise faith. But our faith or lack of it doesn't change God's power.

We also need to realize that God rarely supersedes His laws of nature. Many people get sick because they ignore God's laws of good health, then they run to Him for healing. If two people, one a Christian and the other not, jump off a thirty-story building, no matter how much the Christian prays on the way down, both will be devasted when they hit the ground. Likewise, we cannot violate God's laws of good health and expect God to keep healing us.

Second, *we need to be cautious of dramatic testimonies*. People often are eager to share about healings, but their experiences do not necessarily prove that God was at work. Often the problem is selection of facts. This is especially true when hearing about a healing through a letter or a secondhand source. The teller easily exaggerates his story or leaves out essential information.

When people share dramatic testimonies, they often imply that they were healed because they had more faith. This can cause those who aren't healed to doubt God.

Joni Eareckson Tada graphically illustrates this struggle. She worked up her faith to believe God that she would walk again. At a special prayer meeting, church elders, pastors and family laid hands on her, anointed her with oil and prayed for her. She described what happened in the following days:

> A week went by ... then another ... then another. My body still hadn't gotten the message that I was healed. Fingers and toes still didn't respond to the mental command, "Move!" *Perhaps it's going to be a gradual thing* [italics are Joni's], I reasoned, *a slow process of steady recovery.* I continued to wait. But three weeks became a month, and one month became two ....
>
> Then came to my mind the ten-thousand-dollar question, the question that is in the mind of so many I've met over the years who have not been healed in response to their prayers—*Did I have enough faith?*
>
> What a flood of guilt that question brings. It constantly leaves the door open for the despairing thought: *God didn't heal me because there is something wrong with me. I must not have believed hard enough.*[4]

After reviewing her doubts, Joni concluded that her problem was not a lack of faith. She realized that God sometimes does heal people in miraculous ways, but it was His decision—His sovereign choice.

Which leads to my final principle. *We need to understand that God sometimes chooses not to heal.* When my wife Aljeana was sick, I wanted to see her healed. My friends prayed for that with us. As we waited, I began to understand why people look to unusual techniques outside of the medical profession in hope of finding relief.

Looking back, I now believe that divine healing would not have been nearly as great a demonstration of God's power. He used Aljeana's victory over pain, suffering and eventually death as a testimony to thousands of people.

Certainly God can and does heal today, but He does not heal everyone who comes to Him, even when they come in faith. Jesus Christ, when He lived on this earth, healed many people. But He did not heal all. Many wanted to be healed but never had the chance. God still loved them and He loves us. We may never understand His workings, but we can rest assured that His individual plan for each one of us is best. Joni explains it well:

> I sometimes shudder to think where I would be today if I had not broken my neck. I couldn't see at first why God would possibly allow it, but I sure do now. He has gotten so much more glory through my paralysis than through my health! And believe me, you'll never know how rich that makes me feel. If God chooses to heal you in answer to your prayers, that's great. Thank Him for it. But if He chooses not to, thank Him anyway. You can be sure He has His reasons.[5]

Charles Swindoll states that God follows a consistent pattern when He chooses to perform a miracle. First, God alone is glorified. Second, there is no showmanship. Third, the unsaved are impressed and brought to the Lord. And fourth, biblical principles and statements are upheld, *not* contradicted.

It is important that we understand what the Bible says about this subject. (It may differ from what we think or hope it says.) James tells us in his epistle, "Is anyone among you sick? Let him call for the elders of the church, and let them pray over him, anointing him with oil in the name of the Lord."[6]

Swindoll explains that, "The specific Greek term used in James 5:14 for anointing does not convey the thought we usually ascribe to it, that is, a religious ceremony in which oil is applied to the head. Here it means to apply or rub something into the skin. In biblical times, oil was used for its medicinal effects on one who was sick. We find this occurring in Luke 10:34 when the Samaritan poured oil and wine onto the wounds of the man victimized by robbers and left for dead. James does not write about ceremonial anointing; what he called for was the use of the best medical procedure of the day . . . then praying. Translating into today's terms, oil represents antibiotics, various other medications, surgery, therapy, and so on."

In that same passage, James says that confession of sin will help with healing. He implies that some are experiencing sickness because of sin. "Therefore, confess your sins to one another, and pray for one another, so that you may be healed."[7]

In summary, I again will say that God does heal today. If He has healed you, rejoice and thank Him. But many are being misled by dynamic personalities who claim to have a gift from God. They may have a gift, but it definitely is not healing. They simply have learned, accidentally or intentionally, some good psychological principles. People need to understand that fact when they go to healing services.

Ultimately, we must realize that God does not serve at our bidding. We see that in the book of Job. After Job lost everything and endured his friends' rebukes, God answered Job, not by explaining His actions, but by giving him a glimpse of Himself. God asks Job question after question: "Have you ever caused the sun to rise in the morning? . . . .Can you lift up your voice and command the clouds to release their rain? . . . Can you satisfy the appetite of a lion and the raven?" On and on He goes, graphically showing Job that he is God.[8]

That is what we need—a glimpse of God. When we see Him, the proper perspective on healing will follow naturally.

Chapter Fifteen

FINDING ULTIMATE REALITY

In Latin America, peasants walk for miles on their knees to prove their repentance. South Sea Island natives stick hundreds of needles in their bodies. In the Philippines, people have their backs beaten raw and sometimes even crucify themselves. African witch doctors drive "magic" pegs into the ground at each corner of a village or hut.

These are just some of the religious rituals I've observed over the years. Each is designed to help people find inner peace with themselves and God. There are eleven major religions in the world today, but almost every week someone invents a new religion or cult. Among the thousands of options, how does anyone know which one is right? And how does Christianity differ from all the other religions?

It is interesting to hear what some of the greatest religious leaders have said. Buddha made this statement to his closest followers shortly before he died: "I have given you all the truth I have known. I have shared with you all the life that I have been given. But there cometh one after me who is a fulfillment of all truth and who is the light of the world."[1] Five hundred years later, Jesus Christ said, "I am the light of the world."[2] No other person in history has made such a fantastic claim, and backed it up with his life.

Shortly before Mahatma Gandhi's death, the great Indian guru reportedly said, "It is a constant torture to me that I am still so far from the one whom I know to be my very life and being. I know it is my own wretchedness and wickedness that keeps me from Him."[3] Jesus said, "I am the way, and the truth, and the life; no one comes to the Father, but through Me."[4]

Of course, not everyone follows the great religions and religious leaders of the world. Some people are atheists. Many have dedicated their lives to political causes, particularly communism. In Latin America, the audiences for my university performances frequently are 50 to 80 percent Communists or Marxists. One former Communist professor said, "Students are Communists not because of conviction, but because of frustration."

I find that most people are frustrated by the emptiness in their lives. Some try to fill that void by pursuing material pleasure. Others seek political power. Some look for popular recognition. Still others pursue sensual pleasures. People then look to religion as an answer to the emptiness they find in such pursuits.

To some, Christianity appears to be little different from other religions. They may view it as a sober lifestyle that takes all the fun out of life. Or they may see it as a long list of rules and regulations. Some see it as a series of steps to heaven, or classes in which the believer hopes to make a passing grade before he dies. Still others see it as a ritual of prayers and ceremonies.

But none of those things are Christianity. Genuine Christianity centers around the gospel, which means "good news." In fact, Christianity is the greatest news ever announced. There are thousands of religions, denominations and philosophies, but only one gospel.

Religion is a process of reasoning by the human mind. The gospel is revelation of the divine mind.

Religion originates on earth. The gospel originated in heaven.

Religion is the story of what sinful man tries to do for a holy God. The gospel is a wonderful story of what a holy God has done for sinful man.

Religion is good views, the opinions of simple men. The gospel is good news, the declaration of a righteous and loving God.

Religion commences by trying to create an outward transformation. The gospel begins by creating an inner transformation.

Religion is based on the teachings of man. The gospel is not based on the teachings of Jesus, but rather His death, burial and resurrection. Jesus did not come to earth to preach the gospel, but rather that there might be a gospel to be preached. As we study the various religions and philosophies of the world, this is where we find the difference. Apart from the gospel, there is no provision for man's sin.

God originally created man to have fellowship with Him, so He gave man a body, soul and spirit. But man chose to go his own independent way, and therefore fellowship with God was broken. This is what the Bible means by the word "sin." In essence, man said to God, "You go Your way, I'll go mine. I can run my own life."

The results of that decision were disastrous. God said that in the day man sinned, he surely would die. But man did not die physically—he died spiritually. I demonstrate this in my shows with a lamp in which the light represents a person's spirit. As a result of man's sin, he is born physically alive, but spiritually dead. He has no light in his life—just a great void or emptiness.

Everywhere I go in the world, people tell me this describes their lives. They feel the emptiness, but most people try to cover it up. As a result they are laughing on the outside, but crying on the inside. They try to fill the vacuum with things like sex, drugs, alcohol, education, materialism and religion, but none of these things can fill it. We can take an empty bottle, put a label on it and say it contains anything we want, but until something is put into it, the bottle is still empty. Our label may say Protestant, Catholic, Muslim, Hindu or Jew, but that does not change the emptiness inside. Without God, man is incomplete.

Everyone shares this common problem, but there is a solution. In John 3, we read about a great religious leader, Nicodemus, who came to Jesus one night. This man was extremely religious. He probably knew the entire Old Testament by heart and prayed seven times each day. He worshipped God in the temple three times daily. Yet despite his devotion to religion, he knew something was missing in his life.

Nicodemus acknowledged that Jesus had come from God. Jesus answered him, "Unless one is born again, he cannot see the kingdom of God."[5] Those words baffled Nicodemus. Then Jesus explained that to experience physical life, you must be born physically. Likewise, to have spiritual life, you must be born spiritually. That turns on the spiritual light in your life. Those who are "born again" become members of the family of

147

God.

John Wesley once was asked, "Why do you spend so much time speaking on the subject, 'You must be born again'?" He answered, "Because you must be born again." If we miss this point, we miss the most important point of the entire Bible. Being born again is the difference between Christianity and religion.

Becoming a Christian is not a process but an event. A story of two law students helps to illustrate it. These students were best of friends in law school. After they graduated, one went on to become a prominent attorney and later a judge. The other took to a life of drinking and gambling, and got into trouble with the law.

One day, the second man was arrested and brought before his one-time friend. Naturally everyone wondered what the judge would do. They were all surprised when he levied the stiffest fine the law would allow. If the man didn't pay it, he would be forced to go to jail. Then the judge surprised the people even more. He stepped down from the bench, took out his checkbook, paid the fine and allowed his friend to go free.

That is what God has done for each one of us. Everyone on earth is born spiritually dead. By nature we are sinners, which means we live our lives independent of God. The only way the light of our spirit can be illuminated is by being born again. And that is possible only because God, in His love, stepped out of eternity into time and visited earth. For thirty-three years He walked this planet, and at the end of that time He allowed the people He created to spit upon Him, beat Him and nail Him to a cross. He came to die on a cross of wood, yet He made the hill on which it stood.

But it didn't end there. Three days later, Jesus was raised from the dead, so that we who were dead in sin could be raised to new life in Him.[6]

The Bible says, "He who has the Son has the life; he who does not have the Son of God does not have the life."[7] A Christian is a person in whom Christ dwells, through the Holy Spirit. People without Christ may be very religious, but they are not Christians.

Perhaps for the first time you understand that Christianity is not a long list of do's and don'ts, but rather a spiritual relationship with the Son of God. You know that if you died tonight, you would not enter the kingdom of God because you never have been born again. The solution is to invite Jesus Christ to come into your life.

Jesus is a gentleman. He will not force His way into your life; He enters only by invitation. If you are ready to receive Him, I invite you to pray a prayer similar to the one I prayed many years ago. God is not so concerned about your words, but the attitude of your heart. He knows if you are sincere in wanting to turn from your sin and to accept the payment He made for you. Here is a suggested prayer:

"Lord Jesus, thank You for dying for my sins. Right now, I invite You to come into my life. Forgive my sins and make my life what You want it to be. Thank You, Lord Jesus, for coming into my life because I asked You to and because You promised that You would. Amen."

If you prayed that prayer, I encourage you to begin reading the Gospel of John, the fourth book of the New Testament. As you read, ask God to make Himself real to you. You will find, as I have, that ultimate reality is found in the person of Jesus Christ.

FOOTNOTES

Chapter One:
1. Psalm 23:4 (King James Version).
2. Kendrick Frazier, "Articles on the Paranormal: Where Are the Editors?" *The Skeptical Inquirer*, Winter 1980-81, p. 2.
3. Ibid., p. 4.
4. "Amityville Hokum: The Hoax and the Hype," *The Skeptical Inquirer*, Winter 1979-80, p. 3.
5. "Paranormal Powers Are So Much Hocus-Pocus," *Science*, January 25, 1980, p. 389.

Chapter Two:
1. John 3:16.
2. Jeremiah 29:13.

Chapter Three:
1. Harry Houdini, *A Magician Among the Spirits*, New York: Harper and Brothers, 1927, pp. 266, 270.
2. Raymond Fitzsimons, "Death and the Magician: The Mystery of Houdini," *Reader's Digest*, July 1981, p. 205.
3. Allen Spraggett and William V. Rauscher, *Arthur Ford: The Man Who Talked with the Dead*, New York: New American Library, 1973, pp. 245, 246.
4. James Randi, *Flim-Flam!* Buffalo, New York: Prometheus Books, 1982, p. 246.
5. Deuteronomy 18:9-12 (Living Bible).
6. M. Lamar Keene, *The Psychic Mafia*, New York: St. Martin's Press, 1976, pp. 147, 148.
7. Isaiah 8:19 (LB).
8. See 2 Corinthians 5:8.

Chapter Four:
1. Taken from *The Beautiful Side of Evil*, by Johanna Michaelsen, Copyright, 1982, Harvest House Publishers, 1075 Arrowsmith, Eugene, Oregon, 97402, pp. 98-100. Used by permission.
2. William A. Nolen, M.D., *Healing: A Doctor in Search of a Miracle*, New York: Random House, Inc., 1974, p. 265.

151

3. Ibid., p. 272.
4. Ibid., p. 274.
5. Ibid., pp. 292, 293.
6. Matthew 7:21-23 (LB).

Chapter Five:
1. Russell Targ and Harold Puthoff, "Information Transmission Under Conditions of Sensory Shielding," *Nature*, vol. 251, Oct. 18, 1974, pp. 602-607.
2. Ibid.
3. Ibid.
4. "Investigating the Paranormal," *Nature*, vol. 251, Oct. 18, 1974, p. 559.
5. Martin Gardner, "How Not to Test a Psychic: The Great SRI Die Mystery," *The Skeptical Inquirer*, Winter 1982-83, p. 34.
6. Ibid., pp. 38,39.
7. James Randi, "The Project Alpha Experiment: Part 1. The First Two Years," *The Skeptical Inquirer*, Summer, 1983, p. 31.
8. Persi Diaconis, "Statistical Problems in ESP Research," *Science*, Vol. 201, July 14, 1978, pp. 131-136.
9. Ibid.
10. "Interview with Dave Hunt," *SCP Journal*, vol. 4/2, Winter 1980-81, p. 4.
11. Luis W. Alvarez, "A Pseudo Experience in Parpsychology," *The Skeptical Inquirer*, Summer 1982, pp. 72, 73.

Chapter Six:
1. *Doctrine & Covenants*, Salt Lake City: Church of Jesus Christ of the Latter Day Saints, 1949, Section 84:114. September 22 and 23, 1832.
2. *Doctrine & Covenants*, December 25, 1832, Section 87:1-8.
3. Oliver H. Huntington Journal, Book 14, 1837 (original in Huntington Library, San Marino, California).
4. Joseph Smith, *History of the Church*, January 4, 1833, Vol. 1, pp. 315, 316.
5. A. Voldben, *After Nostradamus*, Secaucus, NJ: Citadel Pr., 1974, p. 54.

6. F.K. Donnelly, "People's Almanac Predictions: Retrospective Check of Accuracy," *The Skeptical Inquirer*, Spring, 1983, p. 49.

7. Ibid., p. 50.

8. Josh McDowell and Don Stewart, *Understanding the Occult*, San Bernardino, Calif.: Here's Life Publishers, 1982, pp. 58, 59.

9. *Doctrine & Covenants*, Salt Lake City: Church of Jesus Christ of the Latter Day Saints, 1949, Section 62:1, 6 and 7.

10. Ibid., Section 84:4.

11. Daniel St. Albin Greene, "The Real Story of Jeane Dixon," *The Christian Reader*, April-May 1974, p. 70.

12. Ibid., p. 71.

13. Ibid., p. 74.

14. Fawn M. Brodie, *No Man Knows My History: The Life of Joseph Smith the Mormon Prophet*. New York: Alfred A. Knopf, 1975, p. 405.

15. Ibid., pp. 457-488.

16. Joseph Smith, *History of the Church*, Salt Lake City: Deseret Book Company, 1957, Vol. 4, p. 461.

17. Josh McDowell and Don Stewart, *Understanding the Cults*, San Bernardino, Calif.: Here's Life Publishers, 1982, p. 96.

18. J. Edward Decker, *To Moroni with Love*, Seattle: Life Messengers, p. 43.

19. "A Psychic Watergate," *Discover*, June, 1981, p. 8.

20. Deuteronomy 18:21, 22.

21 Ray Hyman, "Cold Reading: How to Convince Strangers that You Know all About Them," *The Zetetic*, Spring/Summer, 1977, p. 21.

22. H. J. Eysenck and D.K.B. Nias, *Astrology: Science or Superstition?* New York: St. Martins, 1982, pp. 12, 13.

23. Ibid., p. 214.

24. Ibid., pp. 215, 216.

25. "A Controlled Test of Perceived Horoscope Accuracy," *The Skeptical Inquirer*, Fall, 1981, pp. 29-31.

26. Isaiah 47:13, 14.

27. Jeremiah 10:2, 3.

28. See Marvin W. Cowan, *Mormon Claims Answered*, Salt Lake City: Marvin Cowan, 1975, pp. 19, 20.

29. See Matthew 24:42-44; 1 Thessalonians 4:13-18.

Chapter Seven:

1. Charles Berlitz, *The Bermuda Triangle*, New York: Doubleday, 1974, p. 11.
2. Ibid., p. 12.
3. Michael R. Dennett, "Bermuda Triangle, 1981 Model," *The Skeptical Inquirer*, Fall 1981, p. 48.
4. Lawrence David Kusche, *The Bermuda Triangle Mystery—Solved*, New York: Harper and Row, 1975, p. 275.
5. Larry Kusche, *The Disappearance of Flight 19*, New York: Harper and Row, 1980, p. 175, 176.
6. Gerald Jones, "UFOs," *The Dial*, October, 1982, p. 10.
7. Jeff Wells, "Profitable Nightmare of a Very Unreal Kind," *The Skeptical Inquirer*, Summer 1981, p. 51.
8. Ibid.
9. Philip J. Klass, *UFOs Explained*, New York: Random House, 1974, pp. 14, 22, 30, 89, 174, 233.
10. Robert Sheaffer, *The UFO Verdict: Examining the Evidence*, Buffalo, New York: Prometheus Books, 1981, pp. 212, 213.
11. *The Disappearance of Flight 19*, p. 172.

Chapter Eight:

1. Peter Blythe, *Hypnotism: Its Power and Practice*, New York: Taplinger, 1971, pp. 6, 7.
2. Ibid., p. 11.
3. Larry Bodine and Douglas Lavine, "Hypnosis in Courts: Still on Trial," *American Way*, April, 1981, p. 24.
4. Philip J. Klass, "Hypnosis and UFO Abductions," *The Skeptical Inquirer*, Spring, 1981, p. 21.
5. Ernest R. Hilgard, "Hypnosis Gives Rise to Fantasy and Is Not a Truth Serum," *The Skeptical Inquirer*, Spring, 1981, p. 25.

Chapter Nine:

1. See Josh McDowell, *Evidence that Demands a Verdict*, San Bernardino, Calif.: Here's Life Publishers, 1979, pp. 15-79.
2. John 2:1-10.
3. John 11:44.
4. Peter W. Stoner and Robert C. Newman, *Science*

Speaks, Chicago: Moody, 1976, pp. 106-112.
5. Matthew 24:3.
6. Luke 21:24.
7. Matthew 24:6, 7.
8. Matthew 24:22.
9. 2 Peter 3:10.
10. Hal Lindsey, *The 1980's: Countdown to Armageddon*, Portland, Maine: West Gate Press, 1981, p. 27.
11. *The World Almanac and Book of Facts 1984*, Newspaper Enterprise Association, New York, p. 698.
12. Lindsey, p. 31.
13. Frederic W. Farrar, *The Life of Christ*, Dutton, Dovar, Cassell and Co., 1897, p. 440.
14. Josh McDowell, *More Than a Carpenter*, Wheaton, Ill.: Tyndale, 1977, p. 89.
15. Ibid., p. 97.
16. John 3:2.
17. Frank Mead (Editor), *The Encyclopedia of Religious Quotations*, Westwood, New Jersey: Flemming H. Revell, 1965, p. 56.

Chapter Ten:
1. Matthew 28:18-20.

Chapter Eleven:
1. Acts 18:9, 10.
2. John 16:7.
3. Ephesians 5:18; 1 John 5:14, 15.
4. 1 Corinthians 2:3, 4.

Chapter Twelve:
1. Karen C. Hoyt, "Is Prayer Magic?" *SCP Newsletter*, Jan-Feb 1984, p. 3.
2. 1 Thessalonians 5:17.

Chapter Thirteen:
1. Hebrews 9:27.
2. Colossians 3:2 (LB).
3. 2 Timothy 4:17.
4. Psalms 116:15 (LB).

5. Luke 16:22.

6. 2 Corinthians 5:1 (LB).

7. 2 Corinthians 5:6 (LB).

8. 2 Corinthians 4:7 (LB).

9. 2 Corinthians 5:8.

Chapter Fourteen:

1. William A. Nolen, M.D., *Healing: A Doctor in Search of a Miracle*, New York: Random House, 1974, pp. 286-7.

2. Ibid., pp. 305-6.

3. Steven S. Gaines, *Marjoe: The Life of Marjoe Gortner*, New York: Harper and Row, 1973, pp. 66-68.

4. Joni Eareckson and Steve Estes, *A Step Further*, Grand Rapids, Mich.: Zondervan, 1978, pp. 124-5.

5. Ibid., p. 155.

6. James 5:14.

7. James 5:16.

8. See Job 38.

Chapter Fifteen:

1. Source unattainable.

2. John 8:12.

3. Source unattainable.

4. John 14:6.

5. John 3:3.

6. See Ephesians 2:5, 6.

7. 1 John 5:12.